犹 太 人 在 上 海

冀朝铸

一九五于 十月 一日

犹太人在上海
THE JEWS IN SHANGHAI

潘　光主编

Editor in Chief
Pan Guang

上海画报出版社

Shanghai Pictorial Publishing House

主　　编：潘　光
副 主 编：周国建
　　　　　邓新裕
　　　　　许步曾

策　　划：张锡昌
责任编辑：刘育文
特约编辑：尔冬强
装帧设计：张苏予
英文顾问：黄天民
　　　　　傅睿哲

Editor in Chief: Pan Guang
Associate Editors in Chief:
　　　Zhou Guojian
　　　Deng Xinyu
　　　Xu Buzeng
Plot: Zhang Xichang
Executive Editor: Liu Yuwen
Guest Editor: Er Dongqiang
Designer: Zhang Suyu
English Advisors: Huang Tianmin
　　　　　　　　David E. Fraser

犹太人在上海

潘　光　主编

上海画报出版社　出版
（上海长乐路672弄33号）
新 华 书 店 上海发行所发行
上海电子出版公司制版
上海市印刷七厂印刷
889×1196毫米　开本16　印张6.5　104面
1995年11月第1版　1995年11月第1次印刷
ISBN7－80530－177－8/J·178
定价：80.00元

前　言

　　我们这本反映上海犹太人生活的画册恰逢第二次世界大战胜利50周年之时问世，具有特别重要的意义。

　　50多年前，当纳粹疯狂迫害屠杀犹太人之时，许多正义之士挺身而出救助犹太难民。瑞典外交官瓦伦堡以颁发外交护照等方式救出了上万名匈牙利犹太人；日本驻立陶宛的领事杉原千亩不顾上级禁令给近2000名波兰犹太难民签发过境签证，使之得以逃脱纳粹的捕杀；描写德国实业家辛德勒保护犹太人的电影"辛德勒的名单"现在更是家喻户晓。然而，当时也有些国家和地区对急需救助的犹太难民关上了大门。它们对每一个挣扎在死亡线上的犹太人的拒绝，等于是扼杀了一个生命。

　　回顾那一段历史，我们可以自豪地说，上海在这场善与恶的搏斗中作出了正确的抉择。当整个"文明世界"将犹太人拒之门外之时，它向犹太难民敞开了大门，为救助他们作了一切可能做的事。

　　这本画册，作为中犹友好的一个佐证，用真实而生动的图片，告诉读者的就是这段难忘的故事，以及犹太人在上海的一幕幕值得留恋的历史。

　　19世纪中叶以后，上海成了大批犹太人的定居地。最早来到上海的是塞法迪犹太人；接着是俄国犹太人；最后是为数众多的来自纳粹统治下欧洲的犹太难民。到本世纪40年代初，在沪犹太人总数已超过3万人，形成了远东最大的犹太社团。他们有自己的宗教公会、犹太会堂、学校、医院、俱乐部、公墓、商会、出版机构、政治团体。

　　塞法迪犹太人来到作为远东经贸中心的"冒险家乐园"上海不久，就显示出他们的经商才能。沙逊、哈同、嘉道理等家族发展尤为迅速，在经济上拥有雄厚的实力，与国际商界和伦敦、纽约的金融中心保持密切的联系，积极支持上海犹太社团开展广泛的政治、文化活动，而且对避难来沪的犹太难民也给了很大的帮助。

　　本世纪初，俄国犹太人经西伯利亚、哈尔滨来到上海，他们初来时一贫如洗，只能做一些小本生意，后来经过自身的奋斗逐步上升为中产阶级，由于人数大大超过塞法迪犹太人，形成了一支积极活跃的社区力量。

　　来上海的犹太人中有众多杰出人才。他们的来到赋予上海犹太社团非凡的创造力和多样性，得以组织积极而生气勃勃的教育、娱乐、体育活动。著名的米尔经学院①400余名师生奇迹般地逃脱了纳粹大屠杀，整个战时都在上海坚持学习。上海犹太人在创办报刊方面取得了突出成绩，从1903年至1949年，有50多种犹太报刊以英、德、法、俄、中、日、波兰、希伯来、意第绪等文字在上海出版。

　　值得一提的是，上海犹太人与中国人民之间的互相尊重、同情和支持。

在历史长河中，中华民族和犹太民族都对世界文明作出了重大贡献。与犹太人一样，中国人民也遭受过深重的灾难。超过3500万中国人在抗击日本法西斯的斗争中伤亡。相同的经历，使中国人民对犹太人民怀有深深的敬意和同情。孙中山先生曾在写给上海犹太社团领袖的信中称："所有热爱民主的人都支持复兴你们伟大而历史上著名的民族，她对世界文明作出了如此重大的贡献，理应在国际大家庭中享有光荣的地位。"在希特勒刚发动反犹运动之时，孙夫人宋庆龄亲率一批中国爱国民主人士赴德国领馆，对此表示了强烈的抗议。

同样，上海犹太人也对中国的民族民主运动和抗日战争给予无私的支持。曾长期在上海居住的莫里斯·科亨担任过孙中山的卫士，是中国人民的忠实朋友，以"双枪科亨"著称。汉斯·希伯，一位从德国来到上海的作家和记者，是第一个在中国抗日战争中牺牲在中国土地上的犹太志愿者。我们还要怀着深深的敬意提到罗生特博士。他作为一名犹太难民于1939年从奥地利来到上海，1941年离开上海参加抗日战争。他在共产党领导的军队里辛勤工作10年，成为获得最高军医职位的外国人。中国人民永远不会忘记他们对中国人民解放事业所作的贡献。

半个世纪过去了，"上海犹太人"和他们的子孙后代如今虽然生活在世界各地，但仍视上海为"故乡城"。他们的精力、创造性和影响已远远超过了他们的人数，而且已成为推动中犹人民之间传统友谊不断发展的重要力量。

愿这本画册能使国内外读者对上海在犹太民族离散史上，特别是在拯救纳粹大屠杀的受害者方面所发挥的独特作用有更好的了解。愿在这座东方大都市度过难忘岁月的"上海犹太人"同上海人民，通过这本画册，建立更深厚的友谊。

潘　光
1995年8月于上海犹太研究中心

PREFACE

The publication of this album on Jewish life in Shanghai on the fiftieth anniversary of the victory of World War II is of great significance.

While the Nazis were frenziedly persecuting and slaughtering Jews in Europe over fifty years ago, some people upholding justice stood up boldly to rescue the Jewish victims of Nazi terror. Raoul Wallenberg, a prominent Swedish diplomat, saved thousands of Hungarian Jews by distributing Swedish passports. Chinue Sugihara, Japan's consul in Kaunas, Lithuania, granted transit visas for more than 2,000 Polish Jews, enabling them to escape from the Holocaust. The true story told by the film *Schindler's List* is now known to all. However, at the same time, the governments of many countries imposed strict restrictions on the entrance of Jewish refugees. Especially after 1938, almost all countries closed their doors to the desperate Jews. Their refusal to accept those people struggling for survival on the verge of death was tantamount to choking living beings.

Viewing what the non-Jewish world had been doing to Jews in retrospect, we, the people of Shanghai, are proud of the fact that when all the civilized world closed its doors to Jewish refugees, Shanghai provided a vital haven and every possible relief for them. The authentic and vivid pictures of this album will tell readers the unforgettable story about the Holocaust survivors in Shanghai and also remind them of the unique history of the Jewish community of Shanghai.

From the middle of the 19th Century, Shanghai served as a focus of Jewish immigration to China. By the end of the 1930s, Sephardic Jews, Russian Jews and Jewish refugees from Nazi Europe in Shanghai amounted to over thirty thousand, forming the largest Jewish community in the Far East. The community had its own communal association, synagogues, schools, hospitals, clubs, cemeteries, chamber of commerce, publications, active political groups(especially Zionist parties).

Sephardic Jews immigrated to the city from British-ruled areas like Baghdad, Bombay and Hong Kong as early as the second half of last century. After entering Shanghai, they soon demonstrated their trading capability and did very successful business. Among them, several notable families like the Sassoons, the Hardoons and the Kadoories became economically strong in Shanghai and even across China. Close ties with international corporations and the financial centers of New York and London enabled the Shanghai Jewish community to support a wide range of political and cultural activities. In the period when the European Jewish refugees swarmed into Shanghai, financial support to them from both Shanghai Jewish business circles and American Jewish organizations like JDC was abundant and vital.

Russian Jews came to make a living in Shanghai via Siberia and Harbin after the pogroms and revolutions in Russia at the beginning of this century. Most of them arrived in Shanghai with hardly any money and struggled to open some small business. As time went by, through their own endeavor, a number of Russian Jews became middle class, and with their ever increasing number, far more than the Sephardic Jews, very soon they were beginning to play an active role in the social life of Shanghai.

There were many outstanding intellectuals and professionals among Jews coming to Shanghai. Their influx infused the Shanghai Jewish community with a singular level of creativity and variety. Enriched by their contributions, the community organized active and vigorous educational, recreational and sports activities. All the teachers and students of Mir Yeshiva, a famous Yeshiva in Europe, some 400 in number, miraculously survived the Holocaust and continued their studies in Shanghai throughout the war. Particularly, Shanghai Jews had extraordinary success in the print media. From 1903 to 1949, more than fifty Jewish newspapers and magazines came out in Shanghai in English, Russian, German, French, Chinese, Japanese, Polish, Hebrew and Yiddish. From 1939 to 1946, more than thirty German, Yiddish and Polish newspapers and magazines were published by Jewish refugees in Shanghai. This intellectual experience would not have even been contemplated by them in their authoritarian countries of origin.

What is especially worth mentioning is the mutual respect, sympathy and support between Shanghai Jews and Chinese people. In history, both the Chinese and Jewish nations contributed so much to the civilization of the world. And Chinese people experienced untold sufferings as Jewish people did. Over 35 million Chinese were killed and wounded by Japanese fascists during wartime. This same experience gave Chinese people deep respect and sympathy for Jewish people. As early as April 24, 1920, in his letter to Mr.N.E.B.Ezra, one of the leaders of Shanghai's Jewish community, Dr.Sun Yat-sen, founder of the Republic of China, wrote: "All lovers of Democracy cannot help but support the movement to restore your wonderful and historic nation, which has contributed so much to the civilization of the world and which rightfully deserves an honorable place in the family of nations. "Soon after Hitler's anti-Semitic campaign started, Madame Sun Yat-sen (Ms.Song Qingling) headed a delegation to meet with the German Consul in Shanghai, and lodged a strong protest against Nazi atrocities. Her delegation included all the important leaders of The China League for Civil Rights: Dr.Cai Yuan-pei, Mr.Lo Shun, Dr.Lin Yu-tang and so on. After the middle of the 1930s, Shanghai witnessed more and more denunciations and protests against anti-Jewish outrages in Europe. The indignation they expressed at German fascists was undoubtedly meant as an inspiration to Chinese people who were strenuously resisting Japanese fascists.

Likewise, Shanghai Jews also gave firm support to the Chinese national-democratic movement and resistance against Japanese aggression. Besides the well-known Morris "Two-Gun "Cohen, who was a faithful friend of the Chinese national-democratic cause, there are some more examples. Mr.Hans Shippe, a writer and reporter from Germany, was the first Jewish volunteer to fall in battle on China's soil during her war against Japanese aggression. He left Shanghai and joined the New Fourth Army in 1939. On November 30, 1941, several days before Pearl Harbor, he died with a gun in his hand in an engagement with Japanese troops in Yinan county, Shandong province. Chinese people erected a monument for him near the battlefield. I should also mention Dr.Jacob Rosenfeld with deep respect. He came to Shanghai from Austria as a Jewish refugee in 1939 and left Shanghai to join the anti-Japanese war in 1941. He served in the ranks of the Communist-led army for ten years, obtaining the highest rank as a foreigner of Commander of the Medical Corps. Chinese people will never forget his great contribution in helping resist Japanese aggression and establish the People's Republic.

Half a century has passed. "Shanghai Jews" and their descendants are now living in all parts of the world. But they still regard Shanghai as their "homecity". Their energy, creativity and influence have gone far beyond their number. Especially, they have become an important force in promoting the development of the traditional friendship between Chinese and Jewish people, between China and Israel, and between two of the oldest civilizations in the world.

Pan Guang
Center of Jewish Studies
Shanghai, China
August, 1995

目 录 CONTENTS

前 言
PREFACE

I 上海犹太社团的形成和发展   1
THE FORMATION AND DEVELOP-
MENT OF THE JEWISH COMMUNITY
IN SHANGHAI

II 大屠杀受害者的避难地   22
HAVEN FOR HOLOCAUST VICTIMS
FROM NAZI EUROPE

III 上海犹太人的政治文化生活   46
JEWISH POLITICS AND CULTURE IN
SHANGHAI

IV 上海——中犹传统友谊不   63
断发展的桥梁
SHANGHAI — THE BRIDGE FOR THE
CONTINUOUS DEVELOPMENT OF
TRADITIONAL FRIENDSHIP BE-
TWEEN THE CHINESE AND JEWISH
PEOPLE

参考书目   87
BIBLIOGRAPHY

后 记   89
ACKNOWLEDGMENTS

I 上海犹太社团的形成和发展

19世纪中叶,当黄河岸边的开封犹太社团逐渐被同化之时,东海之滨的黄浦江畔却出现了一个新的犹太社团,其形成的标志便是塞法迪犹商集团在上海的兴起。塞法迪犹太人来自英国统治下的巴格达、孟买、新加坡、香港等地,大都是商人和实业家。当英帝国发动鸦片战争打开了中国大门之后,沙逊家族便来到上海设洋行经商办实业,随之洋行职员及家属陆续抵沪,大都是原籍巴格达的塞法迪犹太人。其中一些人,如哈同、嘉道理等,后来又离开沙逊集团自立门户。他们很快便显示出经商才能,利用与英国各属地的密切联系和上海优越的地理位置发展进出口贸易,迅速积累了巨额财富,随即又投资房地产、公用事业及制造业,逐渐成为上海滩上最为活跃的工商财团。沙逊家族凭借其富厚的家底,很快成为上海犹商财团盟主。而哈同则凭借其精明过人的经商头脑,由初到上海时的一名小职员,发展为南京路上的地产大王,一度被称为远东最富有的人。到本世纪初,在沪塞法迪犹太人约有800~1000人,形成了团结紧密的社团。

这时,由于大批俄国犹太人为逃避俄国的反犹暴行及革命引起的内战而来到上海,出现了近代以来犹太人移民上海的第二次高潮,使上海犹太社团迅速扩大。俄国犹太人比巴格达来的犹太人穷,只能经营餐馆、杂货铺、面包房、时装店、书店等中小型生意,后经奋斗逐步致富而成为中产阶级。

到本世纪30年代中,由塞法迪犹太人和俄国犹太人组成的上海犹太社团发展到5000余人。随着大批欧洲犹太难民的抵达,到1941年底,上海犹太人总数已近3.1万,成为远东最大的犹太社团。直至二战结束后,因犹太难民纷纷返回恢复了和平的欧美各地,上海犹太社团的人数才开始下降。

I The Formation and Development of the Jewish Community in Shanghai

When the old Jewish community in Kaifeng on the bank of the Yellow River was assimilated, a new Jewish community began to emerge on the bank of the Huangpu River in the second half of last century. The mark of the formation of the latter was the rise of Sephardic Jewish (Baghdadi origin) merchants in Shanghai. Soon after the British Empire opened the door of China as a result of the Opium War, the Sassoon family came to the city to open branches of its firms. This led to a steady flow of clerks and their families to Shanghai. Later, however, some of these families such as the Hardoons and the Kadoories established their own independent firms. Using the advantage of close connections with their business partners in British-ruled areas, they acquired great wealth by developing import and export trade. Then they invested in real estate, public utilities and manufacturing, and became the most active industrial and commercial-financial group in Shanghai. At the beginning of this century, there were 800-1,000 Sephardic Jews living in Shanghai.

The second phase of the history of the Jewish community in Shanghai started around 1900 when a new, mainly Russian, wave of Jewish immigration expanded the community. These new arrivals, who had left Russia because of the bloody pogroms and civil war which resulted from revolution, were much poorer than the Baghdadi Jews. They earned their living mainly as small shopkeepers and managed to run restaurants, groceries, bakeries, bookstores, millinery shops and so on. Gradually, through their bitter struggle and hard work, most of them became rich and began to live a life which was considered middle class in the Jewish community.

In the middle of the 1930s, the social life of the Shanghai Jewish community, which numbered 5,000 souls, both Sephardic and Ashkenazi (Russian), was well organized. After Central-European Jewish refugees flowed into Shanghai, the city saw a sudden increase of Jewish residents. Before Pearl Harbor, Shanghai Jews amounted to over thirty thousand. Soon after the end of World War II, the population of the Jewish community began to decrease when a number of refugees left Shanghai.

1. 座落在南京路尽头、外滩边上的沙逊大厦(今和平饭店)。它曾是塞法迪犹太富豪沙逊家族在远东的标志。

2. 和平饭店内景。

1. Sassoon Building (today's Peace Hotel) at the end of Nanjing Road near the Bund. It was the symbol of the Sassoon family in the Far East. (All photos without credits are from the editors' collection and the departments concerned.)

2. Inside rooms of Peace Hotel.

1

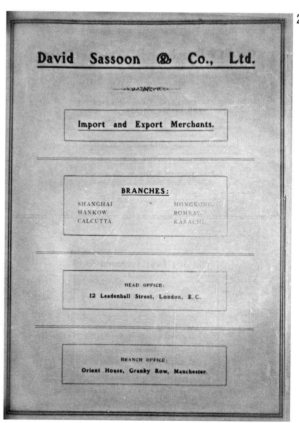

2

1. 维克托·沙逊爵士(1881～1961),上海犹太人社团领袖之一,1920年后一直是新沙逊洋行的首脑。

2. 戴维·沙逊父子公司("老沙逊洋行")于1845年在上海开设分公司。这是公司的广告。

1. Sir Victor Sassoon, 1881-1961, one of the leaders of the Shanghai Jewish community, head of E.D.Sassoon & Co., Ltd. ("New Sassoon Group") since 1920.

2. David Sassoon and Sons Company ("Old Sassoon Group") set up its branch in Shanghai in 1845.

1

1. 西摩路(今陕西北路)犹太会堂,这是J·沙逊为纪念他的夫人而建造的,于1920年落成。

2. 1933年西摩路会堂编印的祈祷书和宗教服务指南。

1. Ohel Rachel Synagogue in Seymour Road (today's Shan Xi Bei Road). It was founded by Sir Jacob Sassoon in his wife's memory, and consecrated in 1920 by Rabbi W. Hirsch.

2. The Book of Prayer and Order of Service edited and revised by Ohel Rachel Synagogue in 1933.

2

THE
BOOK OF PRAYER
AND
ORDER OF SERVICE

According to the Custom of the
SEPHARDI JEWISH CONGREGATION

EDITED AND REVISED
by

THE REV. MENDEL BROWN B. A.
Minister of Ohel Rachel Synagogue

SHANGHAI

5693--1933

סדר התפלות

כפי מנהג ק״ק ספרדים של בית הכנסת

אהל רחל בשנגהאי

עם תרגום אנגלי

הוגה בעיון נמרץ ודיוק היטיב
מאת ר׳ מנחם מענדל ברוין יצ״ו
חכם הכולל דק״ק

שנגהאי

שנת: בכל המקום אשר אזכיר את שמי

אבוא אליך וברכתיך לפ״ק

1. 赛拉斯·阿隆·哈同(1851？～1931)，上海著名的塞法迪犹太人。一度被称为上海的地产大王。他与中国政界和文化界的许多人有交往。

2. 哈同花园是赛拉斯·哈同于1909年建造的，作为哈同家的寓所达30年之久。1954年被拆毁。

3. 博物院路(今虎丘路)上的阿哈龙犹太会堂系由哈同捐资于1927年建成，二战期间米尔经学院师生曾在此会堂内苦读。1985年被拆毁。

1. Silas Aaron Hardoon, 1851?-1931, notable Baghdadi Jew in Shanghai. At the beginning of the 1930s, he was reputed to be the richest Jew in the Far East. He cultivated numerous relations with Chinese political and cultural circles.

2. Hardoon Garden was built by Silas A. Hardoon in 1909. It was the Hardoons' house for three decades and demolished in 1954.

3. Beth Aharon Synagogue in Museum Road (today's Hu Qiu Road). It was established by Mr.Silas A.Hardoon in 1927 and housed the Mir Yeshiva during World War II. The synagogue was demolished in 1985.

1. 埃利·嘉道理爵士(1867～1944)，他是上海塞法迪犹太人社团有影响的领袖之一，1915～1928年间是上海犹太复国协会的主席。

2. 埃利·嘉道理爵士及夫人劳拉·嘉道理之墓。1984年中国政府重修此墓，现嘉道理家属每年都来此扫墓。

3. 大理石宫(今中福会少年宫)由埃利·嘉道理爵士于1924年建造，1924～1949年间为嘉道理家族的寓所。

1. Sir Elly Kadoorie, 1867-1944, one of the influential leaders of the Baghdadi (Sephardi) Jewish community in Shanghai, President of Shanghai Zionist Association, 1915-1928.

2. The grave of Sir Elly Kadoorie and his wife, Lady Laura Kadoorie. Members of Kadoorie family come to visit the grave every year.

3. Marble Hall (now the Shanghai Children's Palace) was built by Sir Elly Kadoorie in 1924. It was the Kadoories' home from 1924-1949.

1

2

3

1. "以色列信使报"第一期。该报不仅在上海，而且在全中国乃至远东都是有影响的犹太报纸。

2. "以色列信使报"的创始人。自左至右：N·E·B·伊斯拉、M·迈耶、I·A·列维斯。伊斯拉是上海犹太人社团的领袖，在1904～1936年间任"以色列信使报"总编辑，1903～1936年间是上海犹太复国主义协会负责人之一。

1. The first issue of *Israel's Messenger*, the influential Jewish newspaper in Shanghai. It had a great impact on Jews of Shanghai, China, and even the Far East for more than three decades.

2. The founders of *Israel's Messenger*. From left to right: N. E. B. Ezra, M. Myers, I. A. Levis. As an active leader of the Shanghai Jewish community, Mr.Ezra was the Chief Editor of *Israel's Messenger*, 1904-1936 and Hon. Secretary of Shanghai Zionist Association, 1903-1936.

1. 艾伯特·爱因斯坦博士和夫人于1922年12月访问上海。1923年1月再次来访。这是他们抵沪时的情景。
2. "以色列信使报"上刊登了他们受到上海犹太社团热烈欢迎的消息。

2

1

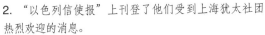

16　　　　　ISRAEL'S MESSENGER

Dr. and Mrs. ALBERT EINSTEIN ARRIVE IN SHANGHAI

ENTHUSIASTIC RECEPTION

RABBI W. HIRSCH and Mr. D. M DAVID PRESENT GREETINGS

BRILLIANT FUNCTION

On Sunday, the 31st December Dr. and Mrs. ALBERT EINSTEIN arrived in Shanghai on the *Hizuno Maru* en route to Palestine and were warmly greeted by the members of the local Jewish community. On board the steamer the visitors were received by Mrs. W. HIRSCH, Messrs. N. E. B. EZRA, S. GATTON and A. E. R. de YONG. An entertainment in their honour was given by the Jewish Communal Association on the 1st instant, at the residence of Mr. and Mrs. S. GATTON, 9 Route Dumer, which was largely attended and proved an unqualified success. The reception Committee who consisted of Messrs. D. M. DAVID, N. E. B. EZRA, S. GATTON and J. E. SALMON left no stone unturned to make the function an unqualified success. At 3.30 p.m. the house of Mr. and Mrs. GATTON which was profusely decorated, presented an animated scene and was crowded by practically the whole community and other prominent non-Jewish residents of Shanghai.

Among those present were: Judge and Mrs. CHARLES LOBINGIER, Dr. and Mrs. H CHATLEY, Mr. A. J. HUGHES, Mr. and Mrs. A. E. de JONGE, Mr. and Mrs. J. FUNATSU, Mr. and Mrs. FRED J. SCHUBL, Mr. D. M. DAVID, Rabbi and Mrs. W. HIRSCH, Mr. DAVID ABRAKI, Mr. J. E. SALMON, Mr. E. SALMON, Mr. and Mrs. N. E. B. EZRA, Mr. and Mrs M. MYERS, Mrs. FLORA EZRA, Mr. H. M. MEYER, Mr. and Mrs. MAX FRIEDMAN, Mr. and Mrs. DAVID ABRAHAM, Mr. and Mrs. VICTOR GESSBERGER, Dr. and Mrs. F. M GESSBERGER, Mr. and Mrs. A. SASHERE, Mr. I. A. LEVIS, Mr. A. E. MOSES, Mr. and Mrs. S. MOOSA,

S. SHPILBERG, Mr. WM. DONALDSON, Mr. WM. KATZ, Mr. E. E. J. ABRAHAM, Mr. SAM PERRY, Mr. and Mrs. I. LION, Mrs. ED. NISSIM, Miss VERA ELIAS, Miss M. PERRY, Mrs. M. SPERLMAN, Mrs. S. J. SHIBETH, Miss ROOZA SHIBETH, Mr. S. SUDKA, Mrs. M. D. IRLIAH, Miss IRLIAH, Mr. NOAH LANDAU, Mr. and Mrs. J. KOPEL MANN, Mr. and Mrs. ELIA SHAM MOON, Mr. S. E. SHAM MOON, Mr. EZRA SHAMMOON, Mr. and Mrs. H. KAMMERLING, Miss KAMMERLING, Mr. DAVID E. LEVY Mr. and Mrs. M. H. ABRADAU, Mrs. R. E. TORO, Mrs. H. FINKEL STEIN, Mr. and Mrs. H. MAGOO Mr. and Mrs. JOHN BERLOWITZ Mr. and Mrs. C. D. KOMAROFF, Mr. L. RADOMINSHULSKY, I. HASSER, F. GOBERNIK, NAIDIS, Dr. R. HOLPPO,

Prof. EINSTEIN speaks German, French and Italian freely and understanding English

1. Dr. and Mrs. Albert Einstein visited Shanghai in November 1922 and again in January 1923. The photo shows they arrived in Shanghai.
2. *Israel's Messenger* reported they were warmly greeted by the Shanghai Jewish community.

1. 1910年，上海塞法迪犹太人社团主席亚伯拉罕先生(左一)与他的家人在寓所花园内合影。

2. 戴维·拉宾诺维奇是上海犹太人社团的杰出人士，犹太杂志"我们的生活"的创始人和编辑。

3. 拉比②梅厄·阿什肯那齐(1891～1954)，上海俄国犹太人的精神领袖，1926～1949年为上海首席大拉比。

4. 摩西会堂位于华德路(今长阳路)，建于1927年，由阿什肯那齐拉比主持。二战期间成为犹太难民的宗教活动中心。

1. Mr.D. E. J. Abraham (first, left), President of the Baghdadi Jewish community in Shanghai, with his family in their home garden in 1910. Courtesy of Yitzhak Sassoon.

2. David B. Rabinovich, prominent member of the Shanghai Jewish community, founder and editor of the Jewish magazine *Our Life*. Courtesy of Rena Krasno.

3. Rabbi Meir Ashkenazi, 1891-1954, spiritual leader of Russian(Ashkenazic) Jewish community in Shanghai, Chief Rabbi of Shanghai , 1926-1949.

4. The original entrance of Ohel Moshe Synagogue in Ward Road (today's Chang Yang Road). The original synagogue was founded by Russian Jews in 1907, and it moved to this site in 1927. The synagogue was headed by Rabbi Meir Ashkenazi and housed many Jewish refugees during wartime.

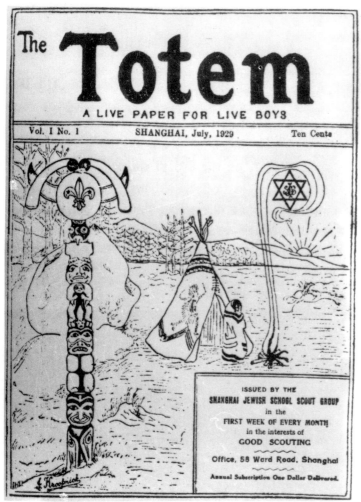

1. 西摩路(今陕西北路)上的犹太学校最初由D·E·J·亚伯拉罕创办于1900年，后迁至现址。该校舍是霍瑞斯·嘉道理于1932年建造的。

2. 上海犹太学校童子军发行的儿童报纸"托腾"。

3. 上海犹太学校的学生于1946年在校舍前的合影。

4. 上海犹太学校1947届毕业生合影。

5. 上海第五(犹太)童子军大队。摄于1932年。

1. Shanghai Jewish School in Seymour Road (now Shan Xi Bei Road). Originally, it was founded by D. E. J. Abraham on the grounds of Sheerith Israel Synagogue in 1900. It moved to Seymour Road in 1932. This school building was founded by Horace Kadoorie in 1932.

2. *The Totem* (Vol. I, No. 1), a boys' paper issued by the Shanghai Jewish School Scout Group. From 13. (See bibliography. The same below.)

3. Pupils of the Shanghai Jewish School in front of school building, 1946. Courtesy of George Reinisch (Sitting in the front row: 2nd from R.)

4. 1947 graduating class of the Shanghai Jewish School. Courtesy of Evelyn Pike Rubin (Sitting: 1st from R.)

5. The 5th Shanghai (Jewish) Boy Scout Troop, cir. 1932. Courtesy of I. Shor.

3

4

5

1. 米勒汽车公司的车队和司机。1939年摄于上海。该公司是由来自哈尔滨的犹太人所罗门·米勒父子创建的。

2. 俄国犹太人格利高里·克莱巴诺夫开在上海静安寺路(今南京西路)的西比利亚皮货店。图为1936年时该店的店面。

1. The fleet of trucks and drivers of the Miller Trucking Company, Shanghai, 1939. The company was established by Solomon Miller and his sons from Harbin. Courtesy of Leib Miller.

2. The Siberian Fur Store run by a Russian Jew, Gregori Klebanov, in Bubbling Well Road (now Nanjing Road, West), Shanghai, 1936. From 12.

1. 毕勋路(今汾阳路)上的原上海犹太俱乐部。

2. 俱乐部内景。

1. The original building of the Shanghai Jewish Club in Route Pichon (now Fenyang Road).

2. Inside decoration of the building.

1. 上海犹太俱乐部理事会成员。

2. 在上海犹太俱乐部举行的第21届哈努卡(犹太"灯节")聚贺会议程表。

3. 上海犹太俱乐部扩建奠基仪式。左四为阿什肯那齐拉比,左十二为犹太社团领导人I·马吉特。

4. 20世纪40年代初上海的俄国犹太人举行的化妆舞会。

1. Board of the Shanghai Jewish Club. Courtesy of Rena Krasno.

2. The front cover of the programme of the 21st annual Hanuccah Ball held in the Shanghai Jewish Club.

3. Laying of Foundation Stone for the extension of the Shanghai Jewish Club. L. to R.: S. Liberman, 2nd and 3rd unknown, Rabbi M. Ashkenazi, V. Zoobitsky, A. Ifland, S. Tomchinsky, Schedzovich, P. Kraslavsky, B. Solomonie, L. Hanim, I. Magid, Jingeroff, S. Hesin, S. Oppenheim, S. Fainland, I. Kagan. Courtesy of Isador A. Magid.

4. Masquerade party held by Russian Jews in Shanghai at the beginning of 1940s. Courtesy of Abraham Fradkin.

3

4

1. 拉都路(今襄阳南路)上的新会堂，是俄国(阿什肯那齐)犹太人社团在1941年建造的。会堂的宗教仪式一直持续至1956年。1993年房屋拆毁。

2. 1934年，塞法迪犹太人出资建造了犹太圣裔社医院。1942年发展成为上海犹太医院(今汾阳路五官科医院病房)。

1. New Synagogue in Rue de la Tour (today's Xiang Yang Nan Road). It was built by the Russian (Ashkenazic) Jewish community in 1941. The services continued until 1956. The synagogue was demolished in 1993.

2. The original building of the Shanghai Jewish Hospital. It was founded in 1942.

ALL STRICTLY "KASHER"

MEAT.	SMOKED and STUFFED.

MEAT.
The fore and leg parts of Cattle
and Sheep.
Tongues, Rumpsteak, Fillets, etc..
VEAL.
SAUSAGE WORKS.
All kinds of sausage.
TALLOW.
The fat tail of sheep larded
and melted.
Geese tallow melted.
Hen tallow melted.
FISH.
The back of dried Nelma and
Carp.
Herrings smoked and marinated.

By special order

SMOKED and STUFFED.
Hen and Duck Stuffed.
Duck and Geese smoked.
Brisket, smoked.
Tongue smoked,
Sheep's Leg smoked.
Rumpsteak Fillet smoked.
SALATS and MARINADS.
Sour Cabbage
Cucumbers salted and
mar nated.
Pickles.
Salted Tomatoes.

According to season

ALL AT MODERATE PRICES
Trial order Solicited

THE PALESTINE Co.

„FIAKER"

Cosy Viennese Cafe-Restaurant

(Ground floor of Weida Hotel)

997 Ave. Joffre   Tel. 78228

Just opened!

Special Viennese & Hungarian Cuisine
under foreign Chef.

"PEPI"

entertains on the piano!

1. 1923年"以色列信使报"上登载的一则"考歇"（犹太教规）食品的广告。
2. 这是霞飞路上由奥地利犹太人开的菲亚克斯餐馆的广告，餐馆的顾客中不仅有外国人，也有中国名人，宋庆龄和宋美龄也光顾过这里。
1. An advertisement about Kosher food in *Israel's Messenger* in 1923.
2. Fiaker Cafe-Restaurant run by Austrian Jews in Ave. Joffre hosted not only foreigners but also Chinese celebrities including Madame Sun Yat-sen and her sister, Madame Chiang Kai-shek. From 5.

1

2

1. 1942年在上海颁发的中国式犹太人结婚证书。

2. 上海犹太文体俱乐部资深会员的会员证。

1. Jewish wedding (marriage) certificate in Chinese style, Shanghai, 1942. Courtesy of Peter Pulver.

2. The Senior Membership Card of the Shanghai Jewish Recreation Club.

1948年末，上海犹太文体俱乐部成员离沪前合影。
Shanghai Jewish Recreational Club sportsmen and functionaries in Hongkew, who were about to leave for Israel, in late 1948. From 13.

Ⅱ　大屠杀受害者的避难地

从1933年到1941年，上海先后接纳了3万多名来自德国及德占地区的犹太难民，除了其中数千人经上海去了第三国外，至1941年12月太平洋战争爆发，仍有25000名左右犹太难民把上海当作他们的临时家园，仅后一个数字就超过了加拿大、澳大利亚、印度、南非、新西兰五国当时接纳犹太难民的总和。

纳粹和他们的帮凶不仅在欧洲杀害了600万犹太人，而且也威胁着欧洲以外的犹太人，如上海犹太社团的生存。1942年7月，太平洋战争爆发后8个月，纳粹盖世太保驻日本首席代表梅辛格上校来到上海，向日本当局提出屠杀犹太人的"上海最后解决"方案。虽然该方案因德日之间的分歧未能实施，但日本当局宣布建立"无国籍难民限定居住区"，强令所有欧洲犹太难民迁入该区。纳粹德国不断施压及日本当局面临失败更趋疯狂，使犹太难民和整个上海犹太社团几度面临险境，然而由于其自身的奋斗及中国人民和全世界犹太人的支援，他们最终逃脱了大屠杀，熬过了战争而幸存下来。

现在，"上海"一词，如"辛德勒"、"瓦伦堡"、"杉原千亩"等名词一样，在有关纳粹大屠杀的史料中已成了"拯救"、"避难地"的代名词。

II Haven for Holocaust Victims from Nazi Europe

From 1933 to 1941, Shanghai accepted over thirty thousand Jewish refugees coming from Europe. Excluding those who left Shanghai for other countries, the city contained a total of 25,000 Jewish refugees as the Pacific War erupted. This means that Shanghai accepted more Jewish refugees than those taken in by Canada, Australia, New Zealand, South Africa and India combined.

The Nazis and their accessories not only killed six million Jews in Europe but also posed serious threats against Jewish communities outside Europe, including the Jewish community in Shanghai. In July, 1942, eight months after the Pacific War broke out, Colonel Josef Meisinger, chief representative of the Nazi Gestapo to Japan, arrived in Shanghai and put forward the plan "Final Solution in Shangha" to Japanese authorities. Although "the Meisinger Plan" was not put into effect due to differences in dealing with Jews between the Japanese and German governments, the Japanese authorities proclaimed "The Designated Area for Stateless Refugees", ordering the refugees who had arrived in Shanghai from Europe since 1937 to move into the area within a month. The pressure of Nazi Germany and the caprice of Japan's policy towards Jews put Shanghai Jews in difficult, unpredictable, and sometimes dangerous straits for nearly four years. But, at last, almost all Shanghai Jews, not only Central European Jewish refugees but also the Sephardic congregation and Russian Jews, survived the Holocaust and war, mainly depending upon their own mutual aid and the great support from American Jews and Chinese people.

Just like "Schindler", "Wallenberg" and "Sugihara", "Shanghai" has now become a synonym of "rescue" and "haven" in the annals of the Holocaust.

虹口犹太难民居住区示意图   The Jewish Rufugee Settlements in Hongkew

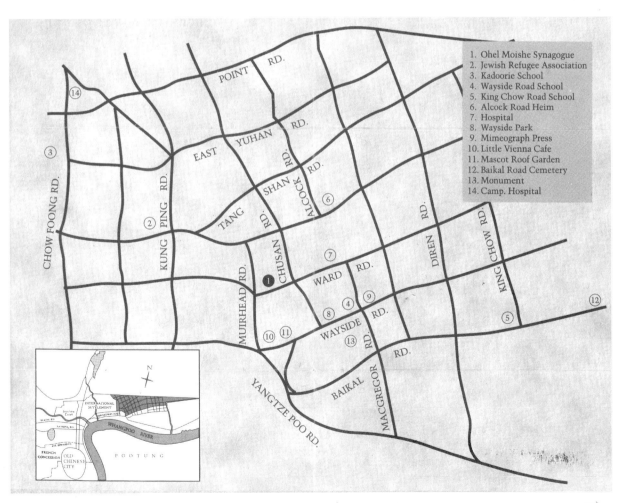

1. Ohel Moishe Synagogue
2. Jewish Refugee Association
3. Kadoorie School
4. Wayside Road School
5. King Chow Road School
6. Alcock Road Heim
7. Hospital
8. Wayside Park
9. Mimeograph Press
10. Little Vienna Cafe
11. Mascot Roof Garden
12. Baikal Road Cemetery
13. Monument
14. Camp. Hospital

THE CIVILIZED WORLD AGAINST HITLERISM

Nazi Germany in the Grip of Medieval Barbarism—Madame Sun Yat-Sen Heads Civil Rights Group in Meeting with Local German Consul—Delegation Calls to Protest Reign of Terror & Frightfulness in Germany—Our Letter of Appreciation

Nazi Germany is having it very hot. The world is moving against it and there can be no question where it stands to-day. Protest against "the brutal terror and reaction prevailing in the realm of Teuton" was entered at the German Consulate on the 13th ultimo, in a group called by the executive committee of the China League for Civil Rights.

Madame Sun Yat-sen headed the delegation and acted as its spokesman in her capacity of chairman. The callers were received by Consul R. C. W. Behrend.

Statements Exchanged

Others present in the delegation included Dr. Tsai Yuan-pei, vice-Chairman of the committee, Mr. Yang Ching, general secretary, Mr. Lin Yu-tang of the *China Critic*, chairman of publicity, the well known Chinese author Mr. Lo Shun, Miss Agnes Smedley, author of the book "Daughter of Earth" and many magazine articles on China, and Mr. Harold Isaacs, editor of the *China Forum*.

A statement conveying the League's views was handed Mr. Behrend, who explained that the consulate was not concerned with political matters but promised that the document would be transmitted to the German Legation. He expressed the view that troubles in Germany have been exaggerated in press reports abroad and that the nation has been an object of adverse propaganda. The callers exhibited clippings from the German press in substantiation of their statement, which read in part as follows:

"Terror In China"

League for Civil Rights protests in the most energetic manner against these facts, report of which are duplicated in all the press of Europe and America. We protest against this fearful Terror against the German working class and progressive thinkers, a Terror which is crippling the social, intellectual and cultural life of Germany."

Our Appreciation

We have forwarded the following letter to Madame Sun Yat-Sen, expressing our sense of gratification over the valiant stand taken by the China League For Civil Rights, in defense of law-abiding minority in Nazi Germany:—

"MADAME SUN YAT-SEN.

"Shanghai.

"DEAR MADAME,—I take the liberty of addressing you this letter, in order to express my appreciation for the step taken on behalf of suppressed and oppressed humanity in the reign of terror and frightfulness in Nazi Germany.

"The China League For Civil Rights has fully justified its existence for the fearless manner in which it has rebuked tyranny and oppression, and I am sure the whole civilized world will applaud the step taken under your leadership to tell the aggressor "Thou art the man."

"Public opinion has long been against the Hitlerite regime, and there are no two opinions that anti-Semitism is the result of error and misconception prompted by bigotry and narrow-mindedness. Its propaganda is intended to divert the discontent of the masses to the Jews who are blamed for all the ills from which the world suffers. A galaxy of Jewish thinkers, philosophers and scientists are to-day languishing in Nazi Germany and their freedom and liberty are restricted and freezed to the point of death.

"Anti-Semitism in Hitlerite Germany is spreading and nothing will suppress it except the voice of civilized nations, who must begin to see in this new movement a menace to the peace of the whole world. Hitlerite Germany has been already arraigned before the bar of civilization and denounced in every land.

"I beg to enclose herein a newspaper clipping showing 100 instances of Hitler's "Policies" committed during the past year. This list has been compiled at the request of the American Jewish Congress and may be taken as authentic and genuine.

"In the hope that your valiant protest may serve to awaken the dormant soul of Germany, I remain, with due respect.—Yours sincerely,

N. E. B. EZRA, *Founder-Editor.*

"SHANGHAI, 15th May, 1933."

1. 宋庆龄(右五)与中国民权保障同盟领导人蔡元培(右四)、鲁迅(右一)、林语堂(右二)等在一起。
2. 1933年5月13日，以宋庆龄为首的一个代表团会见了德国驻上海领事，对纳粹在德国的暴行表示强烈抗议，代表团成员包括蔡元培、鲁迅、林语堂等。"以色列信使报"在1933年6月2日报道了此事。

1. Madame Sun Yat-sen (3rd from L.) and some leaders of The China League for Civil Rights: Dr.Cai Yuan-pei (4th from R.), Mr.Lo Shun (1st from R.), Dr.Lin Yu-tang (2nd from R.).
2. On May 13, 1933, Madame Sun Yat-sen (Ms.Song Qingling) headed a delegation which met with the German Consul in Shanghai, Mr.R. C. W. Behrend, and lodged a strong protest against Nazi atrocities in Germany. *Israel's Messenger* reported the protest on June 2, 1933.

1938～1939年，犹太难民涌入上海的高峰期

1938-39 ----- peak years in which Jewish refugees from Nazi Europe swarmed into Shanghai.

1. 再见吧，柏林！1939年，罗森菲尔德全家离开德国赴上海。

2. 纳粹德国发给犹太难民的护照，上面"目的地"一栏将"伊拉克"改为"上海"，说明上海当时在接收犹太难民方面的重要地位。

1. Good-by Berlin. The Rosenfelds on their way to Shanghai in 1939. Courtesy of Ingeborg Wiener (nee Rosenfeld).

2. The passport of Carl Israel Flatow, a Jewish refugee coming to Shanghai from Germany. It was issued by Nazi Germany in 1940. Note change of destination on p.3 from Iraq to Shanghai. Courtesy of Ziffer family.

1

2

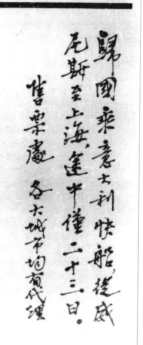

LLOYD TRIESTINO

Nach Ostasien

mit den beliebten Express-Schiffen

D. „Conte Verde"
18 800 to

D. „Conte Rosso"
17 800 to.

M.S. „Victoria"
13 000 to.

Reisedauer:

Italien-Hongkong 21 Tage
Italien - Shanghai 23 Tage

Auskünfte und Buchungen
bei den Agenturen der Gesellschaft

in Deutschland:

Berlin, Unter den Linden 24

Frankfurt a. M.   **Hamburg**
Kaiser Strasse 20   N. Jungfernstieg 17

München   **Stuttgart**
Odeons Platz 1   Schiller Platz 4

in China:

Shanghai   **Hong-Kong**
„Hamilton House"   Queen's Building,
170, Klangse Road   Corner Connaught Road
                              and Ice House Road

und bei den bedeutendsten Reisebüros.

歸國乘意大利快船，徑威尼斯至上海途中僅二十三日。售票處　各大城市均有代理

1. 意大利轮船公司的广告。许多犹太难民乘坐这家公司的轮船来沪。
2. 犹太难民们走下轮船。
1. Advertisement of Italian Lloyd Triestino Company. Many refugees from Nazi areas came to Shanghai by ships of this company. From 6.
2. Refugees disembarking.

1. 他们登上卡车。
2. 志愿人员开车把他们送到接待中心。
1. Refugees loaded on trucks.
2. Volunteers drove refugees to one of the processing
centers.

1. 河滨大楼在1938年曾作为犹太难民接待站。

2. 大批行李堆积在收容所外。

3. 平凉路收容所容纳200人的大房间。

4. 援助欧洲来沪犹太难民委员会（CFA）主席米歇尔·斯皮尔曼。

5. 美犹联合救济委员会(JDC)为救助难民，在上海设立办事处。这是办事处旧址。

6. CFA的领导成员合影。

1. Embankment building was one of the processing centers for refugees in 1938.

2. Luggage of new arrivals on grounds of Chaoufoong Road Heim. From 1.

3. This dormitory in Pingliang Road Heim slept 200 new arrivals. From 16.

4. Michel Speelman, Chairman of the Committee for Assistance of European Jewish Refugees in Shanghai (CFA).

5. American Jewish Joint Distribution Committee (JDC) set up its office in Shanghai for assisting refugees. This building was JDC's office in 1938.

6. The leadership of CFA.

4

5

6

1

Shanghai Hebrew Relief Society
and
Shanghai Hebrew Shelter House
and
Jewish Women's Benevolent Society
JOINT COMMITTEE:

EXECUTIVE COMMITTEE:

Mrs. R. E. Toeg—Chairman
Mrs. Linda Notrica—President (absent)
Mr. H. Kammerling—Act. President
Mr. S. Liberman—Vice President
Mr. S. Oppenheim—Hon. Treasurer
Mr. J. D. Godkin—Hon. Secretary

GENERAL COMMITTEE:

Mrs. M. Z. Ashkenazi—Vice President
Mrs. H. Kammerling—Vice President
Mrs. H. Barukhson
Mrs. G. R. Baylin
Dr. H. Brick
Mrs. M. Buchman
Mr. Solomon Fein
Mrs. Haim
Mrs. J. Haim
Mrs. M. Kahan
Mrs. H. Klebanoff
Mrs. B. Kopeliovich
Mrs. P. Leibovitch
Mrs. J. Malchinsky
Mrs. M. Rabinovitch
Mrs. S. Rubinraut
Mrs. B. Topas
Mrs. S. Toukatchinsky

The Shanghai Hebrew Relief Society
and SHELTER HOUSE

Activities during 1940 at a glance

Monthly Allowances given
to 36 Families

Temporary Assistance given
to 72 Families

Passages paid for Repatriation
of 8 Families

MEDICAL ATTENDANCE
HOSPITALS FEES
MENTAL WARDS

Total Expenditure:

Shanghai Hebrew Relief Society $16,394.25
Shelter House   -   -   - $46,309.61

Comparison of Expenditures:

Grand Total of Expenditure for		1935	-	-	$20,743.27
"	" "	1936	-	-	$21,022.98
"	" "	1937	-	-	$23,554.00
"	" "	1938	-	-	$26,757.15
"	" "	1939	-	-	$34,518.33
Grand Total of Expenditure for 1940			-	-	**$62,703.86**

1. 1940年时上海希伯来救济会及收容所的领导成员名单及其活动情况。该会在救济犹太难民工作中发挥了巨大作用。
2. 佐拉赫·瓦尔哈夫蒂格(摄于1993年),1962至1974年间任以色列宗教部长。他曾于1941年来到上海,为使滞留立陶宛和日本的波兰犹太难民进入上海做了大量工作。他在《难民和幸存者》一书中详叙了在上海的经历。

1. The leadership and activities of the Shanghai Hebrew Relief Society and Shelter House in 1940.
2. Zerah Wahrhaftig (photo taken in 1993), an influential leader of the Mizrahi movement and member of the Israeli Cabinet (for religious affairs) from 1962 to 1974, came to Shanghai in 1941 as a refugee from Poland. After stopping in Shanghai for two months, he went to the United States before Pearl Harbor. In his book *Refugee and Survivor*, he described his experience in Shanghai.

1. 著名的米尔经学院的师生们奇迹般地逃脱大屠杀的魔爪，从欧洲来到上海。图示师生们在上海阿哈龙会堂内继续学习。

2. 一个来自德国的犹太难民的孩子正在开始学一门新的语言——希伯来语③。

1. The Mir Yeshiva, a famous Yeshiva in Europe, miraculously escaped from the Holocaust and came to Shanghai. Beth Aharon Synagogue was the study hall of the Mir Yeshiva in Shanghai. Courtesy of Rabbi S.M.Kalmanowitz.

2. German Jewish child acquired a new language --- Hebrew.

1. 校长露茜·哈特维希。
2. 嘉道理学校是由霍瑞斯·嘉道理于1939年在虹口创办的。该校的大部分学生是难民子弟。
3. 嘉道理学校的学生正在上课。

1. Lucie Hartwich, Headmistress of the SJYA School. From 14.
2. The Shanghai Jewish Youth Association (Kadoorie) School in East Yuhang Road. It was founded by Sir Horace Kadoorie in Novenber 1939 in Hongkew. Courtesy of Horst Eisfelder.
3. The classroom of the SJYA school. Most students were refugee children. From 17.

1. 嘉道理学校的成绩报告单。课程中包括希伯来语。

2. 嘉道理学校的演出节目表。

3. 犹太难民组织——中欧犹太协会的代表们合影。

1. The SJYA School Report. Among the subjects was Hebrew. From 6.

2. The playbill of the SJYA School.

3. The representatives of the Jewish community of Central European Jews.

1
3

PROCLAMATION
Concerning Restriction Of Residence and Business of Stateless Refugees

(I) Due to military necessity places of residence and business of the stateless refugees in the Shanghai area shall hereafter be restricted to the undermentioned area in the International Settlement:

East of the line connecting Chaoufong Road, Muirhead Road and Dent Road;

West of Yangtszepoo Creek;

North of the line connecting East Seward Road, Muirhead Road and Wayside Road; and

South of the boundary of the International Settlement.

(II) The stateless refugees at present residing and/or carrying on business in the districts other than the above area shall remove their places of residence and/or business into the area designated above by May 18, 1943.

Permission must be obtained from the Japanese authorities for the transfer, sale, purchase or lease of the rooms, houses, shops or any other establishments, which are situated outside the designated area and now being occupied or used by the stateless refugees.

(III) Persons other than the stateless refugees shall not remove into the area mentioned in Article I without permission of the Japanese authorities.

(IV) Persons who will have violated this Proclamation or obstructed its enforcement shall be liable to severe punishment.

**Commander-in-Chief of the
Imperial Japanese Army in the Shanghai Area.**

**Commander-in-Chief of the
Imperial Japanese Navy in the Shanghai Area.**

February 18, 1943.

1. 1943年2月18日，日本当局宣布建立"无国籍难民限定居住区"，命令自1937年以来从欧洲抵达上海的难民在一个月内迁入这一地区。

2. 上海阿什肯那齐合作救济协会(SACRA)于1943年2月28日建立，以处理所谓"无国籍难民"进入虹口隔离区事宜。图为委员会成员合影。

3. 约瑟夫·梅辛格上校，系纳粹盖世太保驻日本的首席代表。他在1942年7月向日本占领当局提出屠杀上海犹太人的"上海最后解决"方案。

1. On February 18, 1943, the Japanese authorities proclaimed "The Designated Area for Stateless Refugees", ordering the refugees who had arrived in Shanghai from Europe since 1937 to move into the area within a month.

2. SACRA--The Shanghai Ashkenazi Collaborating Relief Association was formed on February 28, 1943 to deal with the problem of relocating the "stateless refugees" to the ghetto in the Hongkew sector of Shanghai.

3. Colonel Josef Meisinger, chief representative of the Nazi Gestapo to Japan. He put forward the plan "Final Solution in Shanghai" to Japanese occupation authorities in July 1942. From 2.

1. 难民在1943年春迁入虹口隔离区。

2. 虹口隔离区内一条难民聚居的小巷。

3. 犹太难民身份证。

4. 犹太难民进入虹口隔离区后，须得到通行证才能外出。这是一张通行证的正面，上面写有允许外出的时间。

5. 这是另一张通行证的背面，上面的地图划定了通行范围。

1. Refugees moving to the Hongkew ghetto in spring, 1943. From 2.

2. An alley in Hongkew. Many of the refugees lived in houses in such alleys. From 12.

3. Jewish refugee identification card. Courtesy of Ziffer family.

4. Front of refugee pass to leave Hongkew Ghetto. Notice the time on it. On bottom right corner is oval stamp with signature of Ghoya (see P.44). Courtesy of Melchior family.

5. Back of another refugee pass to leave Hongkew Ghetto. Notice map. From 15.

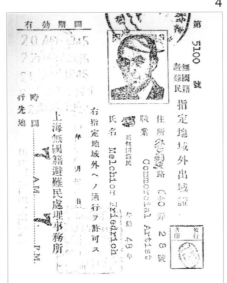

Refugee member of the Pao Chia checks the pass of another refugee returning to the ghetto. (Courtesy: H. P. Eisfelder)

海軍警備地區保甲事務所
NAVY PAO CHIA OFFICE
上海共同租界工部局警察
SHANGHAI MUNICIAPL POLICE

戶口調查表
PAO CHIA CENSUS FORM

上海無國籍避難民就・轉・退職許可證
THE PERMISSION FOR
New Employment · Change of Employment · Retirement
Shanghai Stateless Refugees Affairs Bureau

許可證番號 Permit No.	1021	日附 Dated	24 MAY 194
雇備主氏名 Employer's Name:		Y & S Kirk	
被雇者氏名 Employee's Name:		Richter Edith	
營業塲所 Business Address:		425/4 Kungping Rd	
住所 Residence:		135/47 Tongshan Rd	
通行證番號 Special Pass No.			
昭和 年 月 日		上海無國籍避難民處理事務所	

1. 犹太保甲在检查通行证。

2. 日本占领当局在虹口组织了"犹太保甲"，强迫犹太青壮年在隔离区担任守卫巡逻工作。图为日本当局印制的中英文户口调查表。

3. 上海无国籍难民事务所颁发的就业、转业、退休许可证。

1. Refugee member of the Pao Chia checks the pass of another refugee returning to the ghetto. From 19.

2. Pao Chia Census Form issued by Japanese Pao Chia office. Pao Chia was an international force which the Japanese had organized in 1942 to police Shanghai. The Hongkew Ghetto gates were guarded by the Jewish branch of the foreign Pao Chia. Courtesy of Isaak Teicher.

3. The Permission for New Employment/Change of Employment/Retirement issued by Shanghai Stateless Refugees Affairs Bureau. From 7.

为生存而奋斗，中犹人民同甘共苦

Struggle for sheer survival: a Jewish boom town in Hongkew.

1. 1941年前后的虹口华德路难民收容所。
2. 华德路收容所的厨房内，犹太难民在准备餐食。摄于1940～1942年间。
3. 难民在虹口拥挤的院子里烧饭。
1. Ward Road Camp Heim, Hongkew, cir 1941.
Courtesy of Horst Eisfelder.
2. Kitchen detail in Ward Road Camp, Hongkew, cir.
1940-1942. Courtesy of Arnold Lacker (3rd from left).
3. Refugees preparing their meals in a crowded
courtyard in Hongkew Ghetto. Courtesy of Arthur
Rothstein.

1. 两位犹太老人用上海式煤炉煮食物。
2. 虹口犹太难民家庭的室内装饰。
3. 犹太难民与他们的中国邻居在虹口东有恒路(今东余杭路)兴旺的集市上。

1. They also learned to make food with a traditional Shanghai-style oven which burns coal briquet. From 22.
2. Interior decoration of a Jewish refugee family's house in Hongkew.
3. Jewish refugees and their Chinese neighbours in prosperous market of East Yuhang Road, Hongkew. Courtesy of Horst Eisfelder.

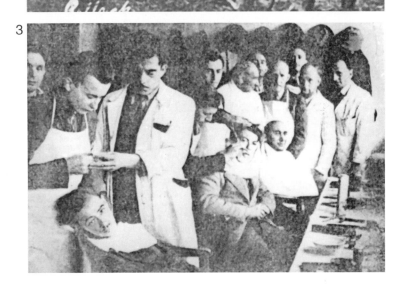

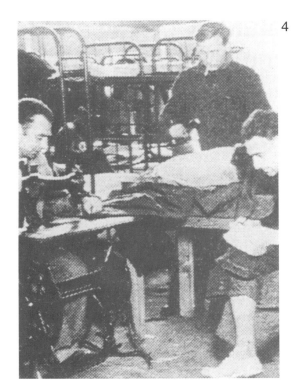

1. 培训就业组织(ORT)战时在上海向犹太难民提供多种技能培训，起了很重要的作用。这是该组织发行的介绍1941～1947年在上海活动的小册子。

2. 木工培训班。

3. 理发培训班。

4. 缝纫、熨烫衣物。

1. ORT (the Society for Promotion of Handicrafts and Agriculture among Jews) played an important role by providing training in a variety of skills to Jewish refugees in Shanghai during wartime. This is ORT's publication about its activities in China 1941-1947.

2. ORT Carpentry Course. From 14.

3. The barber school. From 16.

4. They were busy working sewing machines. From 22.

1. 40年代初舟山路上的维也纳咖啡馆。
2. 舟山路市场熙熙攘攘的人群，这里是虹口隔离区的商业中心。
3. 公平路上一家犹太人开的杂货店。

1. Vienna Cafe Restaurant in Chusan Road. From 6.
2. Chusan Road Market was the commercial center of the Ghetto. Courtesy of Horst Eisfelder.
3. Hans Lowenstein's Grocery in Kungping Road. Courtesy of Robert Kats.

1. 在虹口罗伊屋顶花园餐厅消夏的人们。

2. 唐山路饭店的外景。

3. 米歇尔·曼弗里德与其家人在他的商店前合影。这张照片摄于1946年他关店歇业赴澳大利亚之前。

4. 华德路的路易斯咖啡店以出售搅奶油而闻名。

1. Roy Roofgarden Restaurant in Hongkew. Courtesy of Horst Eisfelder.

2. Tongshan Restaurant and Provision Store. Courtesy of Horst Eisfelder.

3. Michel Manfred and his family in front of his shop in Seward Road. This photo was taken before they closed the shop and left for Australia in 1946. Courtesy of Michel Manfred.

4. Whipped cream made by Cafe Louis in Ward Road was very famous. Courtesy of Horst Eisfelder.

1. 1943年虹口收容所俱乐部乒乓赛
冠军。
2. 犹太难民在做体操。
3. 虹口爱尔考克路(今安国路)收容所
内举行的戏剧表演。

1. Table Tennis Champions of Seward (Jewish refugee) Camp Club in Hongkew in 1943.
Courtesy of Robert Katz.
2. Gymnastics on (Jewish) refugee "Heim" grounds in Hongkew. Courtesy of Horst
Eisfelder.
3. Theater performance at the Alcock Heim stage in Hongkew. Courtesy of Ursel Joshua.

1

2

4

3

1. 1944年在虹口华德路上举行的一次防空灭火演习。

2. 1945年7月17日，美军飞机误炸虹口隔离区，造成难民死亡31人，伤250人。

3. 空袭后留下的断垣残壁。

4. 周家嘴路犹太公墓一角。这是上海4所犹太公墓中最晚建造的一所，建于1940年，主要安葬犹太难民。

1. Fire fighting drill (against air raid) in Ward Road, Hongkew, cir. 1944. Courtesy of Horst Eisfelder.

2. On July 17, 1945, American aircraft accidentally bombed Hongkew Ghetto, causing the death of 31 refugees with 250 refugees injured. Courtesy of Peter Pulver.

3. After the air-raid. Courtesy of Peter Pulver.

4. Section of the Point Road Jewish Cemetery. This, the last of the four Jewish cemeteries in Shanghai, was established in 1940. Courtesy of Horst Eisfelder.

Ghoya I.

The former King of Hongkew

1

2

3

1. Caricature of Ghoya, the Japanese head of Hongkew Ghetto ("The King of the Jews"). From 5.
2. Ghoya distributing passes to the refugees who earned their living outside the ghetto. From 12.
3. Mr.Max Scheidlinger (center) and his friend (left) who beat Ghoya after the war. Courtesy of Rena Krasno.

44

1. 1945年9月7日，"我们的生活"杂志发表文章祝贺盟军获得二战胜利。

2. 首批美军军官于1945年8月18日抵达嘉道理学校。后排右侧两人是嘉道理兄弟。

3. 1946年，上海的犹太难民正在细读大屠杀幸存者的名单，寻找他们亲属的名字。

1. A greeting article was published in *Our Life* on September 7, 1945 for Allied Victory. Courtesy of Beth Hatefutsoth Museum of the Jewish Diaspora.

2. The first group of US Army officers visited the Jewish Youth Association School on August 18, 1945. The Kadoorie brothers are behind the officers on the right. Courtesy of Horst Eisfelder.

3. Refugees looking through lists of Holocaust survivors for names of their relatives, Shanghai, 1946. From 20.

Ⅲ　上海犹太人的政治文化生活

历史上, 在上海乃至全中国从未出现过反犹主义。当然, 一些白俄、日本法西斯分子和纳粹党徒曾在上海、哈尔滨等地搞过反犹活动, 但那不是在中国土地上自发产生的, 也没有对中国人的生活产生过重大影响。

没有反犹土壤的大都市上海为犹太社团的社会生活提供了有利条件。特别在租界内比较宽松的环境中, 犹太社团的政治活动十分活跃, 代表了从空想社会主义到犹太复国主义修正派的几乎所有政治倾向。当然, 作为犹太民族的精神支柱, 犹太复国思想在上海犹太人中占主导地位。

上海犹太社团的文化活动亦相当活跃。上海早在19世纪末就已成为中国的文化中心。犹太裔教师、编辑、记者、作家、演员、画家、音乐家和运动员们来到上海后十分活跃, 充分发挥了他们的聪明才智。他们向孩子们传授知识, 组织剧团, 建立流动图书馆, 甚至成立了乐团和足球队。他们办了那么多报刊杂志, 其中"以色列信使"、"我们的生活"、"斗争"、"上海犹太早报"("上海回声")、"犹太呼声"、"意第绪年鉴"等在远东乃至全球犹太人中均具影响。许多犹太文化艺术名人在上海辛勤耕耘, 达到了其创作生涯的高峰。

III   Jewish Politics and Culture in Shanghai

In history, no indigenous anti-Semitic activity has ever taken place in Shanghai, even in the whole of China. We use the word "indigenous" because there had been some anti--Semitic activities in Shanghai and Harbin in the years from 1920s to 1940s, but they were all carried out by White Russian and Japanese anti--Semitists, and later German fascists. We call it "imported" or "imposed" anti--Semitism. It had never emerged naturally and spontaneously from Chinese soil, nor had it exerted any substantial influence on Chinese lives.

Shanghai, free of native anti-Semitism, afforded a hospitable environment for Jewish life. In this free environment Jewish political activities were very lively and ran the entire ideological spectrum, from Utopian Socialism to Revisionist Zionism. As the spiritual pillar of the Jewish nation, Zionism was undoubtedly the dominant movement within Shanghai Jewry. Though the Zionist scene in Shanghai reflected recent developments in the West, its uniqueness was also evident. The conflicts among different Zionist groups were limited in Shanghai. They succeeded in finding common ground on major issues while reserving differences on minor ones.

In addition, the Jews of Shanghai also enjoyed a prosperous cultural life. Shanghai became China's cultural center as early as the late 19th Century. After entering Shanghai, Jewish teachers, editors, journalists, authors, performers, painters, musicians and sportsmen quickly swung into action and soon demonstrated their outstanding capabilities. They taught children, organized drama groups, established circulating libraries, even set up bands and soccer teams, and ran many publications. Some Shanghai Jewish publications, such as *Israel's Messenger*, *Our Life* (*Unser Leben-Nasha Jhisni*), *Tagar*, *Shanghai Jewish Chronicle* (later *Shanghai Echo*), *The Jewish Call*, *Yiddish Almanach*, *Shanghai Woche* and so on, exerted a great influence on Jews not only within China but also in Diaspora communities abroad.

1. 雷蒙·埃利亚斯·托伊格夫人是本世纪20~30年代上海犹太复国运动的领导人之一。

2. 鲍里斯·托帕斯,上海阿什肯那齐犹太社团的领导人。

3. 朱迪丝·本-埃利泽(娘家姓哈撒),上海犹太社团青年领袖,女活动家,曾与日本当局作过坚决抗争。

4. 朱迪丝·哈撒两岁时与中国保姆在一起。

1. Mrs.Raymond Elias Toeg, one of the leaders of the Shanghai Zionist movement in 1920s and 1930s.

2. Boris Topas, leader of the Shanghai Ashkenazi Jewish Communal Association, founder of the Shanghai Zionist Organization "Kadimah". Courtesy of Genny Topas.

3. Judith Ben-Eliezer (nee Hasser), active leader of Zionist movement, especially Zionist-Revisionism in Shanghai. From 8.

4. Judith Hasser aged two with her Chinese "amah" in the summer. From 8.

1. 1931年在上海建立犹太青年组织
"贝塔"的一批年青人。站立者自左至
右：P·萨姆索诺维奇，V·费尔德斯
坦，L·哈宁，J·哈撒，M·马吉列夫，
D·哈宁，M·巴赫。坐者自左至右：L·
科托维奇，H·因伯格。
2. 上海"贝塔"犹太青年组织于1936年
合影，其中R·斯洛斯曼等人于1941年
参加英军对日作战，斯洛斯曼(坐者左
四)牺牲于缅甸。
3. 犹太呼声是由上海犹太青年组织
"贝塔"在1933年创办的英文月刊。

1. The founders of Shanghai Betar in 1931. Standing L. to R.: P. Samsonovich, U. Feldstein, L. Hanin, J. Hasser, M. Morguleff, D. Hanin, M. Bach. Sitting L. to R.: L. Kotovich (main founder), H. Emberg. From 9.

2. Shanghai Betar "Yamit" Group (1936). Sitting (L. to R.): I. Shor, A. Katznelson, E. Hasser, R. Slossman, B. Greenberg, I. Altshuller. Standing: E. Polotsky, D · Frank, V. Shneerson, B. Shafran, Perelman, A. Mille, A. Furman, A. Uvadieff, E. Fomil, S. Shornick, I. Frank, A. Miller, Y. Medavoy. Some of them joined British forces in 1941. R. Slossman lost his life in Burma. From 13.

3. *The Jewish Call*, Zionist - Revisionist monthly in English, was founded in 1933 by Shanghai Betar.

1. "以色列信使报"庆祝创刊25周年专辑。

2. 奥西·列文，上海德文犹太刊物的杰出编辑，上海欧洲犹太艺术家协会主席，上海德奥犹太人的领导者和活动家。

3. "上海犹太早报"（1945年11月后改名"上海回声报"）是上海历时最久的德国犹太人报纸（1939～1949），由奥西·列文创办和编辑。

1. The silver jubilee issue of *Israel's Messenger* on 5 April, 1929.

2. Ossie Lewin, prominent editor of German Jewish publications in Shanghai, Chairman of European Jewish Artists Society (EJAS), active leader of German-speaking Zionist organizations. From 15.

3. *Shanghai Jewish Chronicle* (name changed to *Shanghai Echo* after November, 1945), longest running German Jewish newspaper (1939-1949) in Shanghai, was founded and edited by Ossie Lewin.

1. 另一份由犹太难民办的德文报纸——"八点钟晚报"
2. 40年代在上海具有很大影响的犹太杂志"我们的生活"。1941年创刊，以英语、意第绪语和俄语出版。
3. 1943年在上海出版的犹太作家短篇小说选。
4. 《流浪的犹太人》是二次大战期间上海出版的许多意第绪文④书籍之一。
5. 1943～1944年的犹太日历，由J·M·埃伦堡在上海印刷发行。

1. Another German newspaper *8-UHr Abendblatt* run by Jewish refugees from Central Europe. From 17.
2. *Our Life*, influential Jewish publication in Shanghai in 1940s, was founded in 1941 and edited in English, Yiddish (Unser Leben) and Russian (Nasha Jhisni).
3. Selected Short Stories By Jewish Authors published in Shanghai in 1943.
4. *Farvoglte yidn (Wandering Jews)*, one of many Yiddish titles published in Shanghai during World War II.
5. Jewish calendar 1943-1944 printed and published by J.M.Elenberg in Shanghai.

3 4 5

1. 英文和俄文双周刊"斗争"是由上海犹太复国主义修正派于1946年创办的。

2. 奥西·列文主编的《上海年鉴1946～1947》（英、德文），其中详细介绍了上海犹太社团的情况。

1. *Tagar*, bi-weekly in English and Russian, was founded by Zionists-Revisionists in Shanghai in 1946. Courtesy of Jabotinsky Institute in Israel.

2. *Almanac-Shanghai 1946/47*, edited by Ossie Lewin.

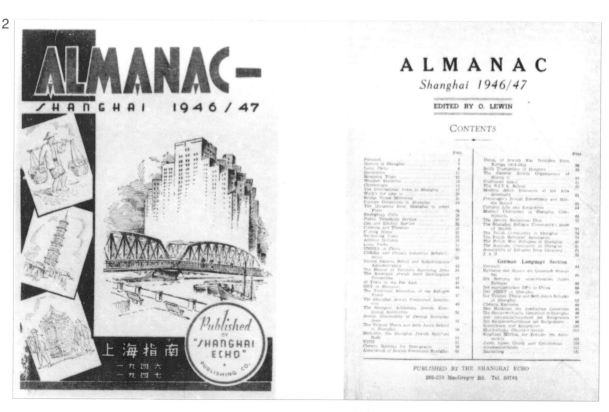

1

2

Zionistische Organisation Shanghai

GEDENKFEIER

anlaesslich des 40. Todestages von

Dr. Theodor Herzl

sowie der Todestage von

Chaim Nachman Bialik
und
Vladimir Jabotinsky.

im Garten des Wayside - Heimes
am Sonntag d. 16. Juli 1944, 6 Uhr abends.

3

1. Betar members holding a memorial service for Jabotinsky, at the Shanghai Jewish Club, 1941. Courtesy of Pana Samsonovich.

2. The public lecture in commemoration of the 40th anniversary of the death of Dr.Theodor Herzl and the death of Chaim Bialik and Vladimir Jabotinsky was held in Wayside Heimes, Hongkew on July 16, 1944. Courtesy of Leon Ilutovich.

3. The local radio, Radio XMHA, offered a variety of programs, including one show hosted by a Jewish refugee, Horst Levin. From 17.

4. Publicity materials made by Shanghai Zionists in English, German and even Chinese, 1945-1947. Courtesy of J.Ben-Eliezer and L.Ilutovich.

1. "贝塔"成员举行悼念雅布廷斯基⑤仪式。

2. 1944年7月16日晚，上海犹太组织在汇山公园⑥内举行报告会，纪念赫茨尔⑦博士逝世40周年以及比亚利克⑧和雅布廷斯基两位已故犹太名人。图为纪念会的海报。

3. 犹太难民H·列维担任了上海XMHA广播电台的节目主持人。

4. 1945～1947年期间上海犹太组织的中、英、德文宣传材料。

4

1. 上海犹太工党领导成员合影于战后初期。

2. 德文"新时日报"上刊载的关于上海犹太复国组织选举出席第22届世界犹太复国大会代表的报道。

3. 里昂·伊路托维奇是上海犹复组织选出参加世界犹太复国大会的代表之一，他是波兰犹太人。

1. The leaders of Jewish Labour Party in Shanghai.

2. *Die Neue Zeit (The New Time)*, German bi-weekly in Shanghai, reported the result of the election of the delegates to the 22nd World Zionist Congress. The election was held in Shanghai on October 27, 1946. Courtesy of Leon Ilutovich.

3. Leon Ilutovich, leader of Polish Zionists in Shanghai, was one of delegates of Shanghai elected to the 22nd World Zionist Congress

1

2

3

1. 1948年4月，虹口"贝塔"成员演出话剧"华沙起义"，图为部分演员合影。

2. 1947年4月19日，上海犹太青年协会编写出版纪念华沙犹太区起义4周年专辑。

3. 1947年4月22日，8000多名犹太人集会，抗议巴勒斯坦的英国当局将4名伊尔贡组织成员处以绞刑。

1. Group of participants presenting the play *The Uprising of the Warsaw Ghetto*. It was presented by members of Hongkew Betar in Shanghai in April, 1948. Courtesy of Sam (Fritz) Gottfried.

2. *Yiskor* commemoration issue for the 4th anniversary of the uprising of the Warsaw Ghetto, published by The Shanghai Jewish Youth Council in Shanghai on April 19, 1947.

3. On April 22, 1947, more than eight thousand Jews gathered to protest the hanging by the British authorities in Palestine of four Irgun members.

1. 莫特卡·奥尔莫特是1929年建立的中国"贝塔"组织的创始人之一，后移居巴勒斯坦成为犹太领导人和农业专家。他1946年再访上海，与犹太组织领导人合影(坐者左四)。

2. 奥尔莫特(坐者左三)与上海犹太妇女领导人合影。

1. Mordechai Olmert (Motia), one of the founders of China's Betar in 1929. After immigrating to Palestine, he became an active leader of Zionist--Revisionism and leading expert in agriculture. He returned to Shanghai in 1946 for assisting in fund raising for Keren Habarzel. M. Olmert (sitting: 4th from L.) with Keren Habarzel Men's Committee. Courtesy of Isador Magid.

2. M.Olmert (sitting: 3rd from L.) with Keren Habarzel Ladies Committee. Courtesy of Isador Magid.

1

TAGAR-
—STRUGGLE
BIWEEKLY
—MAGAZINE

Organ of the United Zionists-Revisionists & Brith Trumpeldor in the Far East

Miss J. Hasser
English Editor
M. Jonis
Russie Editor

Editorial offices of Tagar are open daily,
except Saturday from 3 to 6 p.m. at the
premises of the United Zionists-Revisionists
and Brith Trumpeldor

MONTHLY
SUBSCRIPTION
CAN. $300/50

Shanghai, May 18, 1948   9 Iyar (5708)   Vol. III. No. 10 (46)

WE GREET JEWRY IN CHINA WITH THE ESTABLISHMENT OF THE
STATE OF ISRAEL

THE State of Israel has been created. This is a brief simple statement, but it stands to mean that Israel's age long dream has at last been realised. It stands to mean that we have emerged from a 2000 year old period of inhuman sufferings and vilest persecution to rise to full nationhood, statehood and independence.

This step into the new era is more than revolutionary. It has no precedent in history. Even much of the galuth, accustomed to sorrow, prayer and dreams, regards almost incredulously this historical phenomenon, and fails to appreciate its full significance and import. But understanding will gradually dawn on them, and as they become conscious of the newly acquired dignity and honour, they will realise that the goal—complete freedom and peace—is yet to be won, and the road to it demands their efforts and strain. For they know that today's achievement has not come through prayer and dreams. It came to us through the sweat and blood of those who had faith in the ideal, courage to embark on the straightforward path and to fight every inch of it.

And at this moment, it behoves those who are reaping the benefits of supreme sacrifices made by idealists to take stock of themselves and ask what have they done to help establish this Jewish state and what are they now doing in the fight for its continued existence and freedom.   J. B.

Therefore I shall indeed believe that out of this land
will arise a new and wonderful generation of Jews.
The Maccabees will return to life.   Dr. Herzl

2

1. I·马吉特在上海犹太俱乐部的聚会上宣读以色列独立宣言。

2. "斗争"杂志上发表的文章祝贺以色列建国。

3. 1947～1949年，"贝塔"和"伊尔贡"的总部就设在这幢建筑物内(已拆毁)。

4. 1948年秋，上海"贝塔"和"伊尔贡"组织派两批人去巴勒斯坦，第一批人由塞穆尔·穆勒(右)率领，第二批人由阿里耶·马林斯基(左)率领。

3

4

1. Mr.I. Magid reading Declaration of Independence of the State of Israel on the grounds of the Shanghai Jewish Club in the presence of members and leaders of the Jewish community. Courtesy of Isador Magid.

2. A greeting article was published in *Tagar* on May 18, 1948-- "We Greet Jewry in China with the Establishment of the State of Israel".

3. This building on the grounds of the Shanghai Jewish Club in Route Pichon was the headquarters of Shanghai Betar and Irgun, 1947-48.

4. Shanghai Betar and Irgun sent two groups of young volunteers to Palestine in the autumn of 1948. The first was headed by Samuel Muller (R.) and the second by Arye Marinsky (L.).

1

1. 摩西·尤瓦尔，1948年任以色列驻纽约领事。他是第一位由以色列政府派到中国的外交官，于1948年12月抵沪。他发出了7000张去以色列的签证。

2. 维利·唐是著名的犹太学者，上海亚洲研究会的创始人，他一生献身于成人教育事业。

3. 上海"贝塔"组织青年运动员于1947年合影。

1. Moshe Yuval, Israeli consul in New York in 1948, the first Israeli diplomat appointed to China. He arrived in Shanghai in December 1948 and issued seven thousand visas for Israel. Courtesy of Isador Magid.

2. Willy Y. Tonn, an eminent Jewish scholar, founder of Asian Seminar in Shanghai. He devoted himself to the cause of adult education. From 21.

3. Shanghai Betar sportsmen in 1947. From 9.

2

3

1

2

3

4

1. 阿龙·阿夫夏洛莫夫(1894~1965)，著名犹太作曲家，出生于西伯利亚，在中国生活了30年，大部分时间在上海。这是他在上海家中招待中国友人。
2. 阿夫夏洛莫夫和他儿子在美国波特兰市，摄于1961年。
3. 描绘当时上海著名的意大利犹太小提琴家及指挥富华(左)和德国犹太大提琴家约阿希姆(右)在演奏的漫画。
4. 著名的犹太小提琴家维腾贝格教授来自德国，后成为上海音乐学院教授，直到去世。
5. 他的音乐会演出节目单。

5

4

1. Aaron Avshalomov, 1894-1965, outstanding Jewish composer. He was born in Siberia and lived in China for thirty years (most time in Shanghai). Aaron (far right) hosting his Chinese friends at his home in Shanghai.
2. Aaron and his son Jacob in Portland in 1961. Courtesy of Charles Niss.
3. Caricature: Italian Jewish violinist and conductor Arrigo Foa (L.) and German Jewish cellist Walter Joachim (R.), Shanghai, 1948. Foa and Joachim lived in Shanghai for a long time.
4. Alfred Wittenberg, a famous violinist and Professor of Shanghai Conservatory of Music. He came to Shanghai from Germany as a Jewish refugee and lived in Shanghai until his death in 1953.
5. The playbill of his concert.

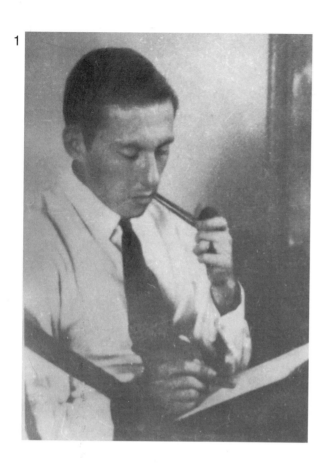

1. 奥地利犹太画家弗里德里希·希夫在上海创作了许多反映中国人民生活的优秀作品。
2. 德国犹太画家白绿黑(Bloch)。
3. 他的展览会"海报"。
1. Friedrich Schiff, a Jewish painter who came to Shanghai from Austria.
2. David Bloch, a Jewish painter who came to Shanghai from Germany. His Chinese name means "white, green, black".
3. A playbill of Bloch's exhibition.

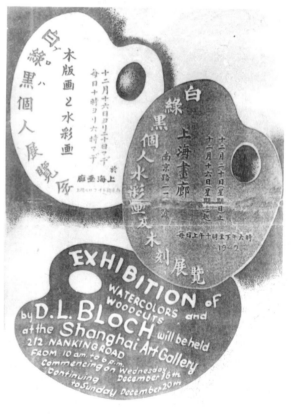

越来越多的有关上海犹太人的著作陆续问世，这里只是其中一小部分。

More and more books and treatises about Shanghai Jews have been coming out. The photos can just show you a very small part of them.

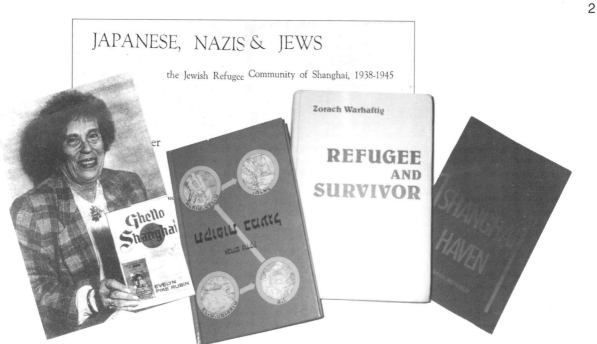

JEWISH REFUGEES
IN SHANGHAI

❖

Published by

THE CHINA WEEKLY REVIEW

SHANGHAI

1. 安娜·金斯伯格的《犹太难民在上海》可能是第一部关于上海犹太难民的专著，出版于1941年。

2. 杨纳·李伯曼的《我的中国，哈尔滨、天津、上海的犹太社团》即将出版，这是本书的宣传单。

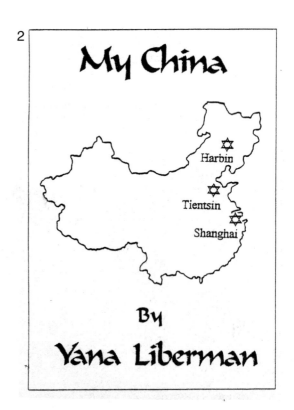

1. Anna Ginsbourg: *Jewish Refugees in Shanghai*. Shanghai, 1941.
This may be the first book about Jewish refugees in Shanghai.

2. *My China* by Yana Liberman will come out soon.

IV   上海——中犹传统友谊不断发展的桥梁

中华民族和犹太民族的文化传统具有许多相同相似之处。如两者都重视家庭纽带和教育功能，两者均吸收了诸多外来文化但主体精神却一以贯之，保持不变。在上海乃至中国从无由文化差异造成的反犹情绪。犹太人定居上海后，与上海居民友好相处，特别在艰苦的战争年代，中犹人民互相帮助，同甘共苦，结下了深厚友谊。在近一个世纪里，上海犹太人吸取了上海文化中许多精华，反过来他们自身的文化传统也对上海产生了影响。在黄浦江畔，许许多多普通的中国人和犹太人共同谱写了中犹友谊史上又一光辉篇章，使上海这座居住着远东最大犹太社团的城市成了促进中犹人民传统友谊的桥梁。

今天，上海犹太社团虽已不复存在，但"上海犹太人"却分布在世界各地。他们的性格、喜好、职业等虽然千差万别，但却有一个共同点——将上海视为"故乡城"，称他们自己为"上海人"。他们为了不忘在上海度过的难忘岁月，纷纷建立联谊组织，经常举行活动，长期保持联系，还出版各类刊物。

他们没有忘记与中国人民结下的友谊。自文革结束后中国实行改革开放以来，他们纷纷携子女亲属来沪寻根、访友，与昔日的中国邻居重聚，在南京路、外滩、虹口流连忘返，为能再尝一口"大饼油条"而兴奋不已。看到上海各行各业高速发展，旧貌换新颜，他们无不欢欣鼓舞。不少人重返"故乡"投资做生意，为上海拓展对外经贸文化联系牵线搭桥，为加速中国现代化建设献计出力。因此，我们可以自豪地说：上海今天仍然是中犹友谊不断发展的桥梁。

IV Shanghai--the Bridge for the Continuous Development of Traditional Friendship between the Chinese and Jewish People

Chinese and Jewish cultures have a lot in common. Both highly emphasize the family tie function and the value of education, and both have absorbed various exotic cultures but their main principles have never changed since birth. For this reason, religious prejudice and racial discrimination against Jews caused by cultural differences do not exist in Shanghai and even throughout China, and never did. After settling down in Shanghai, Jews established friendly relations with the natives of Shanghai. Especially in the hardest days during wartime, Shanghai Jews and their Chinese neighbors enjoyed mutual help and shared weal and woe. In nearly one century between the 1850s and 1950s, the culture and tradition of immigrant Jews drew upon and were enriched by the host city -- Shanghai. They also exerted their influence on the culture of Shanghai. All the factors mentioned above turned Shanghai into the bridge for the promotion of traditional friendship between Chinese and Jewish people.

Although the Jewish community in Shanghai no longer exists, the Shanghai Jews are now scattered all around the world. Their dispositions, hobbies and professions might be varied, but there is one thing in common -- all of them still regard Shanghai as their homecity and call themselves "Shanghaiers". In order to remember the years they spent together in Shanghai, they established a number of reunion organizations in their new settlements and held activities at regular times to keep up close relations with each other. They don't forget the support they received from the Chinese people during their stay in Shanghai. Since China embarked on its road to reform and openness after the end of the Cultural Revolution, many of them have come back with their offspring to look for their roots in Shanghai and visit their old Chinese friends. Some have also established new economic and cultural connections with Shanghai, and even invested in Shanghai to do business.

We are very proud that today's Shanghai continues to be the bridge of traditional friendship between the Chinese and Jewish people.

1. 莫里斯·科亨(1887～1970),1922～1925年间任孙中山先生的副官。孙中山先生去世后,他曾为多位中国领导人工作,升任中国军队中的犹太籍将军。1949年后,他也是中华人民共和国的亲密朋友。他不论到何处总是身佩两把手枪,博得了"双枪科亨"的外号。

2. 汉斯·希伯(右)(1897～1941),德国犹太作家兼记者,1939年参加新四军,1941年11月牺牲于山东沂南县。

3. 中国人民为希伯建立的纪念碑。

1. Morris Cohen ("Two-Gun Cohen"), 1887-1970, aide-de-camp to Dr.Sun Yat-sen, 1922-1925. Following Sun's death, he worked for a series of Chinese leaders and rose to become a Jewish general in the Chinese Army. He was also a close friend of the People's Republic after 1949. He got the name "Two Gun" because wherever he went, he always had two pistols ready for use. From 8.

2. Hans Shippe (R), 1897-1941, a writer and reporter from Germany, the first Jewish volunteer to fall in battle on China's soil during her war against Japanese aggression.

3. Memorial plaque for Hans Shippe on a monument erected on July 7, 1944. It reads: "For the internationalist cause he worked in Europe and Asia, shedding his blood in the Yimeng Mountains in battle against the Japanese invaders."

1

Dr. Jakob Rosenfeld

1. 罗生特(1903～1950)，1939年从奥地利来上海的犹太难民，1941年离沪参加抗日战争，在共产党领导的军队中工作达10年之久，曾任解放军纵队卫生部长，1950年去以色列探亲时因病去世。

2. 从左至右：刘少奇、罗生特、陈毅，1941年4月摄于苏北。

1. Dr.Jacob Rosenfeld, 1903-1950, a Jewish refugee who came to Shanghai from Austria in 1939. He left Shanghai to join the anti-Japanese war in 1941 and served in the ranks of the Communist-led army for ten years. He obtained the highest rank of Commander of the Medical Corps as a foreigner in Chinese army. From 5.

2. From L. to R.: Mr.Liu Shaoqi (later became President of People's Republic of China), Dr.Jacob Rosenfeld, General Chen Yi (later became marshal and the Foreign Minister of PRC), in Jiangsu (North), China, 1941. Courtesy of Shen Qizhen.

2

1. 威廉·迈因策尔医生(1909～1984)与夫人的合影。他是德国犹太人，曾参加抗日战争，成为中国军队中的一位高级医官，1949年，与他的中国妻子移居以色列。现迈因策尔夫人仍住在海法。

2. 上海市人民政府卫生局颁发给俄国犹太人戴维·伯恩斯坦医生的行医许可证，摄于1951年11月。

3. 弗里德里希·希夫的漫画"我爱中国人"。

1

3

2

1. Dr.Wilhelm Mainzer, 1909-1984, a Jewish doctor who came to Shanghai from Germany. He joined the anti-Japanese war and became a high medical officer in Chinese army. He and his Chinese wife immigrated to Israel in 1949. He died in 1984. Mrs.Mainzer lives in Haifa now. Courtesy of S. Gottfried.

2. Certificate of Medical Practitioner for Dr.David Burshtein issued by Shanghai People's Government in November, 1951. Courtesy of Eve Kramer (nee Burshtein).

3. F. Schiff's caricature: *I Like the Chinese*. From 5.

"上海犹太人" 今天生活在世界各地
"Shanghai Jews" live in all parts of the world

1. 朱迪丝·本—埃利泽在以色列拉马特甘家中。
2. 已故劳伦斯·嘉道理勋爵生前曾在香港会见本书主编潘光教授。勋爵1985年访问中国时受到邓小平的接见,他为大亚湾核电站建成投产作出了巨大贡献。
3. 利奥·哈宁,77岁,曾长期生活在上海,现居洛杉矶,仍对中国一往情深。

1. Judith Ben-Eliezer at her home in Ramat-Gan, Israel.
2. The late Lord Lawrence Kadoorie met Prof. Pan Guang in Hong Kong in 1989.
3. Leo Hanin aged 77 in Los Angeles.

1. 伊沙多尔·马吉德，当年上海犹太社团领导人之一，现住在澳大利亚。他为本画册贡献了珍贵的照片。

2. 40年代上海犹太工党的领导人之一耶契尔·多贝基勒现住在纽约。

3. 耶路撒冷希伯来大学从事中国研究的著名教授埃利斯·约菲，他在上海长大。

4. 西奥多·考夫曼是以色列前中国居民协会主席，在促进上海犹太社团研究上起了重大的作用。

5. 约瑟夫·图钦（原名图钦斯基），在上海长大，现在纽约联合国担任重要职务。

1. Isador Magid in Australia. He contributed valuable photos to this album.

2. Yechiel Dobekirer, one of the leaders of the Zionist Labor Party in Shanghai in 1940s, now lives in New York.

3. Ellis Joffe, Professor of Chinese Studies at Hebrew University of Jerusalem.

4. Theodore Kaufman, President of Igud Yotzei Sin in Israel (Association of Former Residents of China), is playing an important role in promoting the research on the Jewish community in Shanghai.

5. Joseph Toochin (Tochinsky) now works for the United Nations in New York.

1. 耶路撒冷米尔经学院的几位"老上海"。

2. 6位出生在上海的犹太难民的子女在萨尔茨堡合影。站者左起：玛丽奥·舒伯特，彼得·芬克格鲁恩，伊娃·格鲁丁。

坐者左起：彼得·克瑞帕斯，索妮亚·缪尔伯格，伊丽莎白·冈尔贝格。

1. "Old Shanghai Hands" of Mir Yeshiva in Jerusalem.

2. Six former refugee children met at the seminar "Flucht nach Shanghai". They were all born in Shanghai. Sitting from L to R: Peter Krips, Sonja Muhlberger, Elisabeth Ganglberger. Standing from L to R: Marion Schubert, Peter Finkelgruen, Eva Ungar Grudin.

1. 1985年上海联谊会在美国纽约举办重聚活动。
2. 1988年上海联谊会在耶路撒冷举办重聚活动的广告。
3. 1995年5月在奥地利萨尔茨堡召开"逃往上海，奥地利犹太人在上海"学术讨论会和重聚活动。图为萨尔茨堡街头的会议布告。

1. 1985 Shanghai Reunion in Kiamesha Lake, New York. From 18.
2. Shanghai Reunion in Jerusalem in 1988. From 7.
3. The International Seminar "Flucht nach Shanghai" in Salzburg, Austria, May 26-28, 1995.

重返 "故乡城"
Returning to "homecity"

1. 美国财政部长M·布卢门撒尔(左三)1979年重访上海，向记者们介绍当年在虹口的旧居。他指出，与他1939年自德国抵沪时相比，一大变化是"街上已没有乞丐和倒毙者"。

2. 布鲁门撒尔1994年再访虹口，会见虹口区区长黄耀金。

1. When Michael Blumenthal (2nd from L.), U.S. Secretary of the Treasury, returned to Shanghai in 1979, he showed off his old Shanghai haunts in Hongkew to the press. One change he noted since he arrived in China from Germany in 1939: "There are now no beggars or people dying in the street."

2. M. Blumenthal met Mayor of Hongkew (now Hongkou) Mr.Huang Yaojing in May 1994 when he visited "homecity" again.

1. 伊瑟·芬克，上海首席大拉比阿什肯那齐之女，
1994年回到"故乡"上海。
2. 阿诺·夏拉马赫和他的妻子访问摩西会堂，阿诺
的父亲1939～1947年是该教堂的首席领唱者。

1. Esther Funk (nee Ashkenazi), daughter of Rabbi Meir
Ashkenazi, visited "homecity" in 1994.
2. Arno Schallamach and his wife visited Ohel Moshe Synagogue. Arno's father was the principal cantor of that synagogue
from 1939 to 1947.

1. 已故以色列前驻联合国大使J·特科阿(中站立者)于1989年回到上海,曾深情地说:"一生中最美好的时光在于青年时代,我在上海度过了青年时代,现在我回来追寻那最美好的时光"。

2. 奥托·斯奈帕,当年犹太难民家一少年,1980年作为美国驻华使馆科技参赞回到上海。他现任美国南加州大学教授,东亚研究院院长。

3. 著名犹太实业家肖尔·艾森伯格曾于1940年逃离德国来到上海。他现在不断扩展在上海的投资,他投资建立的耀华—皮尔金顿玻璃厂是中国办得最成功的合资企业之一。这是黄菊市长会见艾森伯格先生。

4. 本·列瓦哥,曾长期生活在上海,现住洛杉矶,已86岁,每年仍回上海"探亲"。

5. 伊夫·克莱默(父姓伯恩斯坦)出生在上海,她回到当年上海旧居,发现"密苏扎"(犹太人门上传统饰物)仍在她当年出生的房间的门上,不禁激动万分。

1. The late Yosef Tekoah (Tukachinsky) said at a banquet when he visited Shanghai in 1989: "The most wonderful time of the life is youth. I spent the time in Shanghai. Now I am back with the purpose of looking for something that is the best."

2. Otto Schnepp, a former refugee boy, returned to Shanghai in 1980 as scientific attache of the U.S.Embassy in Beijing. He is now a Professor at the University of Southern California.

3. In 1992, the Mayor of Shanghai Huang Ju met Shaul Eisenberg, President of Eisenberg Group of Companies, who escaped from Germany to Shanghai in 1940. Mr.Eisenberg is now planning to expand his investment in Shanghai. The Y.P. Glass Factory, one of his investments in Shanghai, is one of the most successful joint ventures in China.

4. Ben Levaco, living in Los Angeles, returns to Shanghai almost once every year. He is 86 years old.

5 Eve Kramer (nee Burstein) returned to her old Shanghai apartment and found the mezzuzah still attached on the door going into the room where she was born.

1994上海犹太人重聚活动
1994 Reunion in Shanghai

1. 虹口原犹太难民居住区说明牌揭幕仪式。

2. 美国犹太名流代表团团长阿瑟·施奈尔拉比及夫人与以色列驻华武官马龙博士在说明牌揭幕典礼上。马龙博士出生于上海。

1. The unveiling ceremony of the Monument for Holocaust Survivors in Hongkew in April 1994.

2. At the unveiling ceremony: Rabbi Arthur Schneier (center), one of the leaders of the Jewish community in New York, Mrs.Schneier (right), General Moshe Marom (left), Israeli Defence and Armed Forces Attache in Beijing, who was born in Shanghai.

1. 沙麟副市长(右三)会见阿瑟·施奈尔拉比及夫人,市外办主任徐兆春(右二),主任助理夏永芳(右一),外交部参赞郁兴志(左一)参加会见。

2. "我们在上海长大,但从没感觉到上海有反犹主义",美国耶希瓦大学副校长戴维·柴斯曼(站立者左)在虹口区政府的招待会上说。他全家离开欧洲经巴拿马于1934年来到上海。

1. Sha Lin, Vice Mayor of Shanghai, met Rabbi Arthur Schneier.

2. "Those of us who grew up in Shanghai felt no anti-Semitism," said David Zysman (standing), vice president of Yeshiva University in New York. His family came to Shanghai from Europe by way of Panama in 1934.

1. 美国亚美公司总经理约瑟夫·甘杰(面向镜头戴帽者)回到二战时住过5年的唐山路818弄,见到了老邻居。阿瑟·施奈尔拉比(右三)握着818弄居民的手说:"辛德勒的名单救了1000多人,而上海拯救了整个犹太社团数万人"。

2. 当年的犹太难民本杰明·菲肖夫(左二)携全家重返上海,在虹口摩西会堂陈列室居然看到了自己50年前身份证的复制品在展出,左一是他夫人,右一、二是他女儿和儿子。

1. Joseph Ganger (5th from L.), who runs a garment business with headquarters in the Empire State Building, returned to Tangsan Road Lane 818 in Hongkew, where his family lived for five years during wartime, and met with former Chinese neighbors. Rabbi Arthur Schneier (3rd from R.) told residents of Lane 818: "Schindler's list saved a thousand lives but Shanghai saved a whole community of many thousands".

2. Mr. and Mrs. Benjamin Fishoff (L.) and their son, Dov, and daughter, Meryl, visiting the former Ohel Moshe Synagogue, now a museum. Mr.Fishoff found his ID certificate from 1941 on display at the museum.

1. 来自中国、美国、以色列、英国、法国、德国、奥地利、香港等国家(地区)的200多名学者及名流参加了"犹太人在上海"国际学术讨论会。

2. 上海犹太居民联合会执行会长拉尔夫·赫希在学术讨论会上发言。他曾随父母于1939年逃离德国来到上海。

3. 1923年出生在上海的瑞那·克拉斯诺说:"撇开国籍不谈,上海就是我的故乡,我生在上海,长在上海"。

1. The International Seminar "Jews in Shanghai" held in Jinjiang Tower Hotel (five stars) was joined by more than 200 attendants from China, U.S.A., Israel, U.K., France, Germany, Austria and Hongkong.

2. Ralph Hirsch, Executive Director of the Council on the Jewish Experience in Shanghai, speaking at the seminar. He escaped from Germany to Shanghai with his parents in 1939.

3. Rena Krasno, a daughter of Russian Jews who was born in Shanghai in 1923, said: " Apart from the nationality, Shanghai is my motherland. I was Shanghai born and Shanghai bred." She returned to Shanghai for the first time in 45 years and gave a speech at the seminar.

1. 龚学平副市长在学术讨论会上发言,左为上海社科院院长,上海犹太研究中心名誉主任张仲礼。
2. 1937年出生在上海的以色列巴里兰大学副校长耶胡达·哈列维在学术讨论会上发言。

1. Gong Xueping, Vice Mayor of Shanghai, speaking at the seminar.
2. Yehuda Halevy, vice president of Bar-Ilan University in Israel, an Iraqi Jew born in Shanghai in 1937, speaking at the seminar on the topic " The Sephardi Jewish Community in Shanghai ".

1. 参加重聚活动的来宾们参观浦东金桥加工开发区模型。

2. 世界各地报刊关于1994上海犹太人重聚活动的报道。

1. Guests visited Pudong New Areas.

2. More and more reports about 94 Reunion in Shanghai have been coming out. Some of them were published in *The New York Times*, *The Wall Street Journal* and so on.

上海继续在促进中犹友谊方面发挥着桥梁作用
Shanghai continues to play the traditional "bridge role" in promoting Chinese - Jewish friendship

1. 中以两国国旗在天安门广场上迎风招展。

2. 第一个关于纳粹屠杀犹太人的展览会于1991年12月在上海举办。成千人参观了展览会。图片所示是展览会入场券的正反面。

3. 1992年1月24日在北京举行的中国与以色列建交文件签字仪式。

1. The national flags of China and Israel are fluttering in Tian An Men Square, Beijing.

2. The exhibition "the Courage to Remember" was held in December 1991 in Shanghai and thousands of people visited it. It exposed the Nazi atrocities in the Holocaust and was the first such exhibition ever held in China. Pictures are both sides of the admission ticket.

3. The signing of the documents establishing relations between China and Israel, Beijing, January 24, 1992.

1. 以色列总统海姆·赫尔佐格在徐匡迪市长(原副市长)陪同下在工厂参观。总统的叔叔曾避难来沪并死于上海。

2. 以色列总理伊扎克·拉宾夫妇参观南汇县农民家庭。

1. In December 1992, accompanied by the Mayor (then Vice Mayor) of Shanghai Xu Kuangdi, Israeli President Chaim Herzog visited a factory in Shanghai. Mr. Herzog's uncle had lived and died in Shanghai. On behalf of the Israeli people, Mr.Herzog expressed his heartfelt thanks to Shanghai for providing a vital haven for Jewish refugees from Nazi Europe.

2. Israeli Prime Minister Yitzhak Rabin and his wife visited a peasant family in Shanghai suburb.

1. 布卢门撒尔1994年再访上海时会见上海市市长徐匡
迪先生(原副市长)。
2. 以色列外长西蒙·佩雷斯(左三)1993年5月访问上海
和平与发展研究所以色列犹太研究中心。
3. 以色列首席大拉比斯洛莫·戈伦(成人左七)与上海希
伯来文幼儿班的学员们在一起。

1. The Mayor (then Vice Mayor) of Shanghai, Xu Kuangdi met Michael
Blumenthal in May 1994.
2. Israeli Foreign Minister Shimon Peres visited the Center for Jewish & Israeli Studies of the Institute for Peace & Development Studies in Shanghai in
May 1993.
3. Rabbi Shlomo Goren (Adult: 7th from L.), former Chief Rabbi of Israel, with
Hebrew class children in Shanghai in December 1993.

1. 1995年4月20日，江泽民主席会见中国人民的老朋友，著名犹太裔专家爱泼斯坦，祝贺他80寿辰。爱泼斯坦曾在上海生活和工作。

2. 以色列首任驻沪总领事摩西·拉姆。

1. On April 20, 1995, Jiang Zemin, President of PRC, met priminent Chinese writer and scholar of Jewish origin, Israel Epstein, at the ceremony marking his 80th birthday in Beijing.

2. Moshe Ram, first Israeli Consul General in Shanghai.

注释

①米尔经学院:欧洲最古老的犹太教
经学院之一。
②拉比:犹太教法学博士、犹太教教
士。
③希伯来语:犹太人使用的主要语言,
现为以色列国语言。
④意第绪语:生活在东欧和中欧、特别
是德国的犹太人使用的一种语言。
⑤雅布廷斯基:犹太复国主义运动内
部修正派领导人。
⑥座落在虹口区原犹太人聚居区汇山
路上的一个小公园(今霍山公园)。

主要参考书目和资料来源

1. 戴维·克兰兹勒:《日本人,纳粹和犹太人:上海犹太难民社团1938—1945》。纽约,1976年。

2. 马文·托卡耶和玛丽·斯沃兹:《河豚计划,二战时日本人与犹太人之间一段不为人知的故事》。纽约,伦敦,1979年。

3. 赫尔曼·迪克:《远东的流浪者和定居者,犹太人生活在中国和日本的一个世纪》。纽约,1962年。

4. 瑞娜·克拉斯诺:《总是陌生人,战时上海的一个犹太家庭》。伯克利,1992年。

5. 戈德·卡明斯基和爱尔丝·约特瑞德:《奥中友谊史》。维也纳,1980年。

6. 弗兰西丝·克瑞斯勒:《德国文化在中国的影响》。巴黎,1989年。

7. 上海联谊会会刊《虹口记事》。美国加州。

8. 朱迪丝·本—埃利泽:《上海失去,耶路撒冷重获》。以色列,1985年。

9. 《贝塔在中国 1929—1949》,纪念贝塔成立50周年文集。以色列出版。

10. 佐拉赫·瓦尔哈夫蒂格:《难民和幸存者,大屠杀期间的拯救努力》。耶路撒冷,1988年。

11. 乔治·莱尼西:《上海避难地》。切尔坦海姆,1984年。

12. 《移居在中国:哈尔滨、天津、上海的犹太社团》,以色列贝思·哈特夫所斯大离散博物馆编,特拉维夫,1986年。

13. 《以色列前中国居民协会简报》。以色列特拉维夫。

14. 奥西·列文编:《上海年鉴1946—1947》。上海,1947年。

15. 赫瑞塔·雷夫勒编:《来自中国的西雅图犹太人(口述史)》。华盛顿州犹太历史协会,西雅图,1989年。

16. 安娜·金斯伯格:《上海犹太难民》。上海,1940年。

17. 詹姆斯·罗斯:《逃往上海,中国的一个犹太社团》,纽约,1994年。

18. 伊夫琳·鲁宾:《上海隔离区》。纽约,1993年。

19. 欧内斯特·哈帕纳:《上海避难所,回忆二战时的犹太隔离区》。内布拉斯加州林肯市,1993年。

20. 纽约依浮研究所上海资料档案。

21. 纽约利奥·贝克研究所上海资料档案。

22. 联合国档案馆上海资料汇集,纽约。

23. 耶路撒冷耶德·瓦谢大屠杀档案馆上海资料汇集。

24. 犹太复国主义中央档案馆上海资料汇集,耶路撒冷。

25. 亚伯拉罕·弗拉特金:《流散生涯》(希伯来文)。以色列,1990年。

26. 阿里耶·马林斯基:《光明和黑暗》(希伯来文)。以色列,1993年。

27. 伊斯雷尔·基彭:《颠簸人生》。澳大利亚,1989年。

28. 《我们的报刊》,世界犹太记者协会会刊。以色列特拉维夫。

29. 《中国和犹太人,展览目录》,哈佛大学图书馆编,1992年。

30. 《贝思·瑞夫卡赫鲁巴维契学校40周年纪念文集》,纽约,1981年。

31. 《向东方》,美国中犹研究会会刊,美国出版。

BIBLIOGRAPHY

1. Kranzler, David. *Japanese, Nazis and Jews: The Jewish Refugee Community of Shanghai*, 1938-1945. Yeshiva University Press, New York, 1976.

2. Tokayer, Marvin, and Swartz, Mary. *The Fugu Plan, The Untold Story of the Japanese and Jews during World War II*. Paddington Press, New York & London, 1979.

3. Dicker, Herman. *Wanderers and Settlers in the Far East: A Century of Jewish Life in China and Japan*. Twayne Publishers, New York, 1962.

4. Krasno, Rena. *Strangers Always, A Jewish Family in Wartime Shanghai*. Pacific View Press, Berkeley, 1992.

5. Kaminski, Gerd, and Unterrieder, Else. *Von Osterreichern und Chinesen*. Europaverlag, Wien, 1980.

6. Kreissler, Francoise. *L'Action culturelle allemande en Chine*. Ed.de la Maison des sciences de l'homme, Paris, 1989.

7. *The Hongkew Chronicle*, Newsletter of The Shanghai Reunion. Van Nuys, California, U.S.A..

8. Ben-Eliezer, Judith. *Shanghai Lost, Jerusalem Regained*. ZBM Printing Press, Israel, 1985.

9. *Betar in China 1929-1949*, Commemorative Anthology for the 50th anniversary of Betar (1923-1973). Israel, n.d..

10. Warhaftig, Zorach. *Refugee and Survivor, Rescue Efforts during the Holocaust*. "Daf Noy" Press, Jerusalem, 1988.

11. Reinisch, George. *Shanghai Haven*. Standard Commercial Printers, Cheltenham, 1984.

12. *Passage Through China, The Jewish Communities of Harbin, Tientsin and Shanghai*. Beth Hatefutsoth, The Nahum Goldmann Museum of the Jewish Diaspora, Tel Aviv, 1986.

13. *Bulletin of Igud Yotzei Sin in Israel (Association of Former Residents of China)*. Tel-Aviv, Israel.

14. Lewin, Ossie(ed.). *Almanac - Shanghai 1946-1947*. Shanghai Echo, Shanghai, 1947.

15. Reifler, Henrietta(ed.). *Seattle Jews from China (oral history)*. Washington State Jewish Historical Society, Seattle, 1989.

16. Ginsbourg, Anna. *Jewish Refugees in Shanghai*. The China Weekly Review, Shanghai, 1940.

17. Ross, James. *Escape to Shanghai, A Jewish Community in China*. The Free Press, New York, 1994.

18. Rubin, Evelyn. *Ghetto Shanghai*. Shengold Publishers, New York, 1993.

19. Heppner, Ernest. *Shanghai Refuge, A Memoir of the World War II Jewish Ghetto*. University of Nebraska Press, Lincoln & London, 1993.

20. Shanghai Collection at the YIVO Institute, New York.

21. Shanghai Collection at the Leo Baeck Institute, New York.

22. Shanghai Collection of United Nations Archives, New York.

23. Shanghai Collection of Yad Vashem Archives, Jerusalem.

24. Shanghai Collection of Central Zionist Archives, Jerusalem.

25. Fradkin, Abraham. *Periods in the Circle* (Hebrew). Israel, 1990.

26. Marinsky, Arieh. *In Light and in Darkness* (Hebrew). Edanim Publishers, Israel, 1993.

27. Kipen, Israel. *A Life to Live*. Chandor Publishing, Australia, 1989.

28. *Our Press*, Bulletin issued by the World Federation of Jewish Journalists. Tel-Aviv, Israel.

29. *China and the Jews, exhibition* catalog. Widener Library, Harvard University, Cambridge, 1992.

30. *Commemorative Anthology for the 40th anniversary of Beth Rivkah Schools Lubavitch*. New York, 1981.

31. *Points East*, A Publication of The Sino-Judaic Institute. Seattle & Menlo Park, U.S.A..

后　记

　　《犹太人在上海》画册经过一年多的紧张编撰，终于面世了，它收集了200多张珍贵照片。参考了有关书籍、杂志、报刊资料五六十种，同时还征集了海外的上海犹太人后裔所珍藏的照片，而各有关方面提供的照片亦使本画册增色不少。

　　我们在此向外交部，上海市人民政府外事办公室，上海市人民对外友好协会，上海市虹口区人民政府表示衷心感谢，没有他们的悉心指导和大力支持，这本画册是不可能问世的。

　　我们也得到了许多个人和组织的各种形式的帮助，在这里特别向以下个人和组织表示深切谢意：金应忠、陆培勇、诺爱米·达利达基斯及其丈夫乔治、伊沙多尔·马吉德、乔治·莱尼西、曼弗雷德·米切尔、爱德华·魏德曼、弗兰克·塞勒格、莉莉·芬克尔斯坦、威廉·舍特曼、亚伯拉罕·弗拉特金、伊斯雷尔·基彭、朱迪丝·本—埃利泽、瑞娜·克拉斯诺、佐拉赫·瓦尔哈夫蒂格、迈克尔·布卢门撒尔、戈德·卡明斯基、马文·托卡耶、玛茜娅·里斯泰诺、安森·莱特纳、斯蒂文·霍奇斯塔德、齐娅拉·贝塔、梅茜、梅耶、丹尼斯·莱文撒尔、马丁·弗赖伯格及其夫人弗蕾妲、亚伦·斯利夫卡、莫顿·芬克及其夫人伊丝特、塞缪尔·施特里克曼、埃胡德·亚里、温迪·亚伯拉罕·拉契尔·阿贝尔、P·萨姆索诺维奇、阿维·尼尔、索妮亚·缪尔伯格、特丝·约翰斯顿、乔纳森·戈德斯坦、马蒂亚斯·克隆、弗雷德·克拉尼奇；澳大利亚犹太博物馆、美国中犹研究会、上海犹太学研究会、以色列贝思·哈特夫所斯大离散博物馆、以色列前中国居民协会、华盛顿州犹太历史协会、上海犹太居民联合会、香港犹太教区联合会、香港犹太历史学会、日本犹太社团。

　　上海画报出版社的张锡昌、刘育文两位编辑及他们的同事对本画册全力支持，精心编辑，我们在这里也向他们表示感谢。

　　由于有那么多的人支持、帮助我们，不可能列举所有的个人和组织，在此只能表示歉意。

　　由于时间及水平所限，难免挂一漏万，望各方专家批评指教。

　　谢谢所有帮助我们的朋友们。

编　者

ACKNOWLEDGMENTS

We wish to express our deep indebtedness to the Ministry of Foreign Affairs, the Foreign Affairs Office of Shanghai Municipality, the Shanghai People's Association for Friendship with Foreign Countries, the People's Government of Hongkou District of Shanghai. This album would not have been possible without their useful advice and great support.

We also received valuable assistance from a number of individuals, organizations and institutions. We are particularly grateful to the following ones: Jin Yingzhong, Lu Peiyong, George & Noemi Dalidakis, Isador Magid, George Reinisch, Manfred Michel, Edward Weidman, Frank Theyleg, Lilli Finkelstein, William Schurtman, Abraham Fradkin, Israel Kipen, Judith Ben-Eliezer, Rena Krasno, Zorach Warhaftig, Michael Blumenthal, Gerd Kaminski, Marvin Tokayer, Marcia Ristaino, Anson Laytner, Steven Hochstadt, Chiara Betta, Maisie Meyer, Dennis Leventhal, Martin & Freda Freiberg, Alan Slifka, Morton & Esther Funk, Shmuel Shtrikman, Ehud Yaari, Wendy Abraham, Rachel Arbel, P. Samsonovich, Avi Nir, Sonja Muhlberger, Tess Johnston, Jonathan Goldstein, Matthias Kron, Fred Kranich; the Jewish Museum of Australia, the Sino-Judaic Institute, Shanghai Judaic Studies Association, Beth Hatefutsoth Museum of the Jewish Diaspora, Igud Yotzei Sin in Israel (Association of Former Residents of China), Washington State Jewish Historical Society, Council of the Jewish Experience in Shanghai, the United Jewish Congregation of Hong Kong, the Jewish Historical Society of Hong Kong, Jewish Community of Japan.

We are greatly indebted to Zhang Xichang and Liu Yuwen, editors from the Shanghai Pictorial Publishing House, and various colleagues of theirs in SPPH for their great interest in this project and excellent editing of the album.

Since so many friends have helped us complete this project, we have to apologize to any we may have omitted.

Thanks to all friends for their kind help.

Editors